"Michael Alcée's intriguing exploration of OCD's gifts offers a new perspective on a disorder often simplistically treated as uniformly negative. *The Upside of OCD* is a provocative read in the best sense and a welcome addition to a growing literature on thriving in an age of flux and angst."

—**Maggie Jackson**, award-winning author of
Uncertain: The Wisdom and Wonder of Being Unsure and *Distracted*.

"Drawing upon his extensive clinical experience and scientific research as well as his musical creativity, Dr. Alcée has written a most unique and highly compelling re-examination of obsessive-compulsive disorder, exploring not only the burdens of this state of mind but, also, its potential benefits. A hugely clever reframing of this aspect of human psychology, I warmly recommend this book to fellow mental health professionals and, indeed, to all members of the general public!"

—**Brett Kahr**, senior fellow at the Tavistock Institute of Medical Psychology in London; visiting professor of psychoanalysis and mental health at Regent's University London; and honorary director of research at the Freud Museum London.

THE
UPSIDE
OF
OCD

THE
UPSIDE
OF
OCD

Flip the Script to Reclaim Your Life

MICHAEL ALCÉE

ROWMAN & LITTLEFIELD
Lanham • Boulder • New York • London

Published by Rowman & Littlefield
An imprint of The Rowman & Littlefield Publishing Group, Inc.
4501 Forbes Boulevard, Suite 200, Lanham, Maryland 20706
www.rowman.com

86-90 Paul Street, London EC2A 4NE

British Library Cataloguing in Publication Information Available

Library of Congress Cataloging-in-Publication Data

Names: Alcée, Michael, author.
Title: The upside of OCD : flip the script to reclaim your life /
    Michael Alcée.
Other titles: Upside of Obsessive-compulsive disorder
Description: Lanham : Rowman & Littlefield, [2024] | Includes
    bibliographical references and index.
Identifiers: LCCN 2024027908 (print) | LCCN 2024027909 (ebook) |
    ISBN 9781538191101 (cloth) | ISBN 9781538191118 (ebook)
Subjects: LCSH: Obsessive-compulsive disorder—Popular works.
Classification: LCC RC533 .A43 2024 (print) | LCC RC533 (ebook) |
    DDC 616.85/22700835—dc23
LC record available at https://lccn.loc.gov/2024027908
LC ebook record available at https://lccn.loc.gov/2024027909

*To my mom and all who shine and shimmer
as you discover the upside.
May this book show who you've been all along.*

CONTENTS

ACKNOWLEDGMENTS

I'd like to thank Jaqueline Flynn, Joanna Wattenberg, Victoria Shi, Jaqueline Plante, Anna Keyser and all the wonderful folks at Rowman & Littlefield who embraced my new ideas and gave them a lovely home. Sometimes you luck out with the perfect combination of freedom and direction, and that's just what I found with this amazing group.

Writing doesn't happen without lots of invisible mentors and benefactors. Thank you, Susan Cain, Nancy McWilliams, Dr. Ramani Durvasula, Scott Barry Kaufman, Maggie Jackson, Wendy Smith, Adam Grant, Brett Kahr, Jill Stoddard, Brad Stulberg, Alicia Munoz, Lawrence Rubin, and Sarah Wilson. Three writers who were constant encouragers are the wonderful Yael Schonbrun, Nicole Pensak, and Gina Simmons Schneider; thank you all for your unwavering support.

There are only a few therapist-writers right now who are looking at OCD from the unique angle written about here, and these two have both been enormously helpful in shoring up my spirits when I felt quite alone in traversing this new territory. Thank you, Rob Fox and Melissa Mose.

Special thank you to those who shared or gave me permission to write about their stories. Cristi López, your artwork and advocacy inspire me; I could talk to you for hours and never get bored. Joe Alterman, your gift of reading the changes on the keys and through your OCD amazes me; thank you for providing the soundtrack to much of my writing (if you don't feel happy after listening to Joe play, check your pulse and bring yourself to the nearest emergency room).

Catherine Benfield, thank you for sharing the heart and wisdom behind your magnificent work and story. Steve Brumwell, thank you for letting me share a sliver of the art that is your short film Waving. Allison Raskin, thank you for the vulnerability you share on every Substack newsletter and the work you do to continually explore every corner of OCD.

A very special thank you to all the clients (in private practice and at Manhattan School of Music) who openly shared their heart-breakingly beautiful stories and opened my eyes to the wonder and wisdom—to borrow a phrase from Maggie Jackson—within OCD.

I learned about OCD in grad school at Fordham University from some of the best. Dean McKay, you never cease to amaze me with your encyclopedic knowledge of all things OCD, psychology, and pop culture; you took a chance by allowing me to explore new territory on my dissertation on OCD, and this book wouldn't be possible without your generous sponsorship. Fred Wertz, you not only introduced me to the best of existentialism, psychoanalysis, and phenomenology, your class led me to Freud's Rat Man case and the beginnings of seeing something more within OCD. Steve Phillipson, thank you for teaching me the creative ins and out of CBT and ERP, and for sharing your passion in helping those with OCD heal and thrive. At Williams College, I was blessed with the incomparable Laurie Heatherington, a professor who showcased—with equal measures curiosity and compassion—how to find the strengths within those who also suffer.

The OCD community of the International OCD Foundation has been of enormous support in helping me test and tune the ideas found here. I am especially grateful to Alexandra Reynolds, Ethan Smith, and Katie O'Dunne. Thank you to Andrew Bland and Division 32's (the humanistic division at the American Psychological Association) wholehearted embrace of my work and to Candela Bonaccorso and Albert Banta at the William Alanson White Institute who both supported and gave me a platform to share and develop the ideas found herein.

Thank you to Monica Christensen at Manhattan School of Music for being superbly gracious and supportive in making sure I had time to make my deadlines and who recognized the special place in my heart for this book.

This book wouldn't have been possible without the love and support of my family. Thank you to my wife Meryl for her love and support throughout this process. Thank you to my son Aidan for inspiring me with his sensitivity, creativity, and sweet mischief. And thank you to my sister, my Uncle Tom, and Paula Melo for being a trio of the best cheerleaders in town.

Finally, thank you to my mother, Alicia Malca Alcée, who taught me how to find the poetry and music in what most other people just pass by. I hope this book does your story justice and showcases even a fraction of the magic found in your work as a therapist.

INTRODUCTION

Claiming the Hidden Upside

If you've always felt there was more to your OCD than your family, friends, or even your therapist have made of it, then this book is for you. Maybe you've felt it around the edges—the sensitivity and creativity that has always trailed and defined you, with its magic, mystery, and unmistakable fire ready to burn you at every turn.

You know the one, the madness that makes you wash your hands forty-seven times, check the stove half a dozen ways, or replay every single argument as if you're on trial. Yeah, this book is for you.

So little has been made of the creativity and life that stirs in you. It's a wild thing. Of course, it hasn't been easy to domesticate. Some might even say it's been impossible. And yet, domesticate it we will. Surprisingly, we'll keep its bite too.

Remember that children's book *Where the Wild Things Are* (Sendak, 1984)? Dressed in a wolf costume and lunging at his dog with a fork, poor Max just wants to eat up the world. He doesn't care to destroy it. He wants to devour it and imbibe its magic. But he also needs balance. By becoming the king of all wild things and returning home to the warm soup left by his loving mother, Max learns how to have his mischief and morals too.

That's what we're going to do. It's not easy to carry the fire of such feelings. It's scary. The crucible of anxiety, guilt, shame, and anger is difficult to befriend let alone contain. It takes us over.

But don't worry. Who do I think I'm talking to? Of course you're going to worry. So am I. *We're* going to worry in a new way and capitalize on your special sensitivity, your hidden fire that is so often misunderstood.

When your OCD starts to get out of control, we'll determine why it keeps playing in a loop like an earworm. Together, we'll decode its hidden messages. Because it's got more secrets than you realize right now, and that's where the fun and creative power lies.

Don't worry, it'll be *our* secret until the experts recognize the value of your OCD too. Thus far they've reduced it to noise to help bring you relief, but in the process, they've become deaf to its music.

Am I glorifying OCD? Not a chance. The upside of OCD isn't OCD itself *at all*. OCD contains all the downsides—the repeated worries, fears, and self-loathing. It's a circle of hell reserved for about 1 to 2 percent of the American population who are least deserving of being held captive there (Brock & Hany, 2023). The upside originates before OCD even hits the scene. It's where we must return to transform it—"it" being the profound sensitivity to feeling, fragility, and fellowship that most never find the words to express.

Your OCD is a result, not a cause. Propelled by more than biology or behavior, OCD springs from a lack of support for the underlying powers that most people with OCD don't even realize they have. Without learning how to harness your unique sensitivity, perceptiveness, and creativity, OCD holds you hostage.

Ironically, much has been done to reify OCD as if it is the true dragon to slay. What if instead of talking about the "dragon" so much, we finally focus on the princess we're trying to save? There you'll find the upside.

Several centuries ago, Japanese artisans developed a practice of mending broken pottery with dazzling gold. Called *Kintsugi*, it is the art of joining together what was previously broken with precious metals (Smith, 2021). It exemplifies the way that mending our brokenness, and accentuating it rather than hiding it, allows us to emerge stronger and to create a unique beauty of our own. Our journey will take the broken pieces—the limiting, disjointed perspectives of OCD as a problematic, wild thing—and join them together with your hidden gold. Together, we'll repair and beautify this beast (Jamison, 2006; Wilson, 2019).

I've studied and practiced the most popular OCD treatments and everything in between to understand each angle of OCD's inner workings. Using this knowledge, I'll show you how to take apart and put together the pieces of your OCD—its upsides and downsides—in ways you've never encountered before. The only gold you'll need is already waiting inside like buried treasure.

Trusting ourselves with OCD is among the hardest things to do because we are perpetually afflicted with doubt—doubt about hurting the ones we love the most, doubt about whether we said or did the right thing, and a malignant worry that requires constant reassurance that everything is good and we're truly okay. Happily, the upside of OCD brings us back to our creative center.

In the pages ahead, you'll meet a singer who perpetually loses and finds her voice, a nonprofit worker who discovers that OCD creates boundaries in a world where she's always on-call, a husband who reclaims the wisdom in his obsessions around the feared illness of his personal trainer wife, a teenager who'd hardly hurt a fly transforms his fears into a superpower, and many other seemingly strange but fascinating ways OCD attempts to wake you up to creative possibilities.

You'll also be introduced to an inspiring painter who channels her obsessions of violence into captivating canvases, a jazz pianist who follows the changes of his OCD on the keys, a filmmaker who uses her keen sensitivity to capture the perfect light, an engineer who discovers how skilled he is at taking emotional specs, a journalist who learns how to stop fact-checking everything, and an actor who discovers how to own his bad self on and off the stage.

OCD comes with surprising capacities for depth, imagination, and nuance. I'll show how these qualities come to life in cases from my practice, in a few cameo appearances by myself, and through stories of notable innovators in science, art, and business——like Charles Darwin, Nikola Tesla, and Franz Kafka. All three of these well-known historical figures wrestled with familiar obsessive-compulsive opponents—doubt and reassurance-seeking, counting compulsions (arithmomania), and overwhelming ambivalences—and yet flipped them into their fullest creative advantage, discovering revolutionary ways to reimagine their pasts, presents, and future worlds.

You're in good company. From actors Maim Bialik, Lena Dunham, Daniel Radcliffe, Amanda Siegfried, Charlize Theron, and Mara Wilson, to comedians Maria Bamford, Howie Mandel, and Howard Stern, and young adult author John Green as well as pop stars Justin Timberlake, Camilla Cabello, and Kelly Rowland, singer, songwriter, and record producer Jack Antonoff, and soccer star David Beckham, many in the public eye today are spreading hope for those who struggle with OCD. I'll share inspiring quotes from their OCD stories along the way to keep your sights on all that you can be and accomplish with and beyond OCD.

I've written this book to be informative, illuminating, and entertaining. But most of all, I hope it helps you see more beauty in your madness and gallops ahead into a conversation about the ways in which you, too, burn, burn, burn so brightly (Kerouac, 2018).

HOW IS THE UPSIDE GOING TO HELP ME?

It's not easy possessing such an open heart and imaginative mind. When you have OCD, you feel keenly and imagine in gruesome detail. Chaos, uncertainty, and death always seem close at hand. They possess you.

Fortunately, it doesn't have to be this way. In the pages ahead, we'll flip the usual script on OCD and showcase how to trust and befriend your open heart and imaginative mind.

The Upside of OCD shows how to carry this lightning in a bottle. You'll discover a healthy, assertive voice you can rely on. Rather than feeling tormented by no-win choices, you'll reconcile your conflicts with self-compassion and find new ways to negotiate them with the ones you love most.

Our work together will lift that hard-to-describe depression that OCD leaves in its wake. You'll be surprised at how much lighter and yet fuller you will feel, and at how much easier it is to resolve issues that trapped you in the past.

In short, you'll feel the freedom that comes with choosing and directing your creative energies rather than being compelled by them.

Great news! It's no longer a choice to take care of others or yourself. You can do both. Now, let's get back your fire!

1. Will this book only help me find the strengths underneath my OCD or will it actually heal my OCD?

   • Both! Our entry point is the upside, but we'll be resolving the downsides of OCD as we move through the process together.

   • Current treatments take an either/or approach to OCD. Either you assign badness to your obsessions and compulsions and see them as an enemy or you won't get better. Either you don't give the time of day to your OCD, or you make the mistake of believing everything your OCD tells you. There's little room to regard OCD as a friend and helper.

   • We'll relate to your OCD as a frenemy. I'll show you how to befriend the bad sides (enemies) and lean into them as messengers (friends) for a more nuanced view of yourself and your relationships. You won't be caught up in the repetitive torture of your OCD because you'll have transformed and translated it into a more empowered and creative version of yourself.

2. There are many subtypes of OCD like contamination, harm/
   responsibility, relationship, health, and scrupulosity OCD. Will
   this book address all of these or is it only geared toward a
   specific OCD subtype?
   - All these subtypes will be addressed and each of the strategies
     laid out will be helpful no matter what variety your OCD
     takes.
   - OCD springs from the same source, and you'll see how your
     inborn sensitivity and environmental conditions play into
     how and why your OCD manifests in your own signature
     way. Stay tuned for examples from a variety of subtypes to
     help with your own personal version of OCD.

3. Why is this approach so different from the two major treatments
   for OCD: cognitive behavioral therapy (CBT) and acceptance
   commitment therapy (ACT)?
   - My approach takes the best of these treatments and mashes
     them up to create something totally new. The upside per-
     spective focuses on your hidden strengths and better ex-
     plains how OCD works from the inside out. It gives you a
     three-sixty-view of OCD so you can negotiate its most dif-
     ficult and subtle moments with ease. You'll have a powerful
     way to deal with your OCD at its worst and capitalize on it
     to bring out your best too.
   - We'll catch the method to OCD's madness together, fo-
     cusing on the questions that have eluded researchers and cli-
     nicians alike: Why does my OCD center around *this* and not
     that, and why does it flare up at *these* particular moments?
   - Between one-quarter and one-half of people with OCD
     turn down requests to do exposure and response prevention
     (ERP), citing difficulties stomaching it (Begley, 2018;
     Ong et al., 2016). This book is written especially for *you*
     because we'll be doing a whole different kind of exposure

and response prevention, one that is more sympathetic to the full range of your emotions and doesn't feel like more senseless suffering.

4. Will learning about the meaning and message within my OCD just provide unhelpful reassurance?
   - Not at all. The approach I'll be taking has a very specific purpose in understanding the meaning and message of your OCD. We'll be tapping into the nuance of your OCD instead of the negativity that OCD tries to pile on you. I'll be showing you how to differentiate between the dirt that isn't worth wasting your time on and the paydirt where you'll find the gold within.

5. Do I have to be an artist or creative type to access the upside of OCD?
   - Not at all! The creativity within OCD is a psychological creativity that will improve your personal and professional life no matter what you do. You can be a teacher, lawyer, plumber, doctor, construction worker, student, or anything else, and you will still tap into the special powers on the upside.

6. Do I need to be in therapy to incorporate these strategies?
   - No, it is more important you learn how to recognize how and why your OCD works the way it does and to tap into its hidden upside. Therapy can support you in this mission but it's not essential.

7. Do I need to stop other ways to treat my OCD like using medication?
   - Not at all. OCD is complex, and I support using everything to help you get to the upside. My purpose is to tell the fuller human story of your OCD so you can own and transcend it.

8. Why haven't I seen this method of OCD treatment before?

- The upside offers a unique synthesis of all that's out there and being newly incorporated to make OCD treatment more humane, holistic, and transformational. It also does something totally novel by reimagining the place of older treatments thought to be ineffective for OCD. In chapter 1, I'll show you why talk therapy for OCD was thrown overboard in favor of the current CBT/ACT models and why revisiting these older treatments helps recover your sunken treasure. Remember that hidden gold? It's yours to reclaim.

Quiz: Have I been Looking for the Upside of OCD? (True or False?)

—I've often suspected that there was something more to my OCD than what's been made of it.

—I've always been very sensitive and empathic to people, and it's felt like a double-edged sword.

—I've often wished to know why I have my particular kind of OCD.

—Conventional exposure and response prevention hasn't worked for me.

—I've often felt like I was a failure in doing OCD treatment.

—I see virtues and strengths within my OCD but I'm afraid others might judge me for that.

—I have often been scared or worried about losing important people in my life.

—I have often had a difficult time believing that my OCD has no meaning whatsoever.

—Even when I have worked on my OCD with ERP, OCD has still nagged at me, and I can't understand why.

—I've often been called "overly sensitive."

The more statements you checked off as "true" above, the more you've intuitively known OCD's hidden upside. It's highly likely you have felt, thought, and noticed it but haven't had the support or words to make sense of it. Fantastic! We're going to bring all these connections together now in a language you can speak fluently. Even better, by getting these upsides in the spotlight on center stage, you'll heal your OCD and capitalize on all these hidden strengths waiting in the wings.

If you didn't check off many or even some of these statements, don't be discouraged. I guarantee that you're going to be even more wowed by how much there is to learn about your OCD. Your recovery is going to make quantum leaps because of it, and you'll never be able to look at your OCD the same way again.

1

OCD REIMAGINED

DECODING THE RIDDLE OF OCD

When I was in third grade, I was gripped by fear that my mother would be killed if I didn't follow orders. From whom and where these were coming was not entirely clear, but I quickly learned to obey. Like the main character John Nash in the movie *A Beautiful Mind* (Howard, 2001), I was being watched, and everything I thought was being monitored for my loyalty to a sinister totalitarian state of which I had now become a new citizen. There was no way out.

Every day at the religious school I attended, this presence whispered in my ear, "She'll be dead when you arrive home if you think something bad."

Trying to live each day with a pure heart became a curse it threw in my face, a way to trap and punish me in the most painful way imaginable. If I failed, this invisible entity would take away the person I loved and needed most in the world—the single mother who protected me as well as the flame of sensitivity within me which the world seemed all too eager to snuff out.

When the neighborhood kids dared me to throw away my Winnie the Pooh bear all too soon, I foolishly gave in and was heartbroken. The next night, Paddington Bear in his blue duffle coat and red bucket hat appeared on my bed. When we returned from the movies, my mother asked about the hopes and fears of the characters because she could see them still percolating in me, as if I was worried about them too. Like a music conductor, she'd encourage me to allow every section of the orchestra of my mind and heart to play out just a little louder, strengthening a confidence in an invisible capacity I could not yet name.

I adored my mother and knew that without her, my sensitivity would be swept away. So, as Abraham did with God in the story of Sodom and Gomorrah, I negotiated with the amorphous all-powerful entity controlling my fate. If I read every word in the prayer book, it might be appeased. If I had an evil thought, I could cancel it out, and if done right, the entity might be mollified.

But in the end, the charges kept returning. No sooner was I absolved of a crime I didn't even know I committed than a new trial restarted. The world was full of impossible binds. Death and doubt resurfaced at every turn.

It wasn't surprising that I developed OCD. My mother had an identical fear of losing her mother at the same age and struggled with contamination OCD, opening doors with tissues, and ever-ready with rubbing alcohol. "It's just my craziness," she'd confess.

One day, a red futon tied to the roof of our car fell while driving along the highway. Pulling over to the side of the road, 10-year-old me peered into my mother's eyes expecting to find terror there. "Michael, the big stuff doesn't scare me. It's the little things that get me, remember?" And with a smile, I helped reattach our precious cargo.

My mother was familiar with an existence as paper-thin as the tissues she carried with her everywhere to ward off germs. Her parents' marriage fell apart shortly after their arrival in New York from the Middle East via Panama, when her mom—my grandmother—became the main breadwinner and caretaker of four young children. Sensing her fragility, my mother stepped in to minister to her.

Seeing my grandmother, a highly educated woman now working behind the counter at a department store to make ends meet, my mother easily noticed the pain—the unspoken sadness, longing, and fear—that others hardly detected. Even my mom's siblings mistook their mother's desire to have joyful holiday dinners as just another form of control, instead of what it really was: a cry for help. *Please eat and show me, not only that you love me, but that somehow God hasn't abandoned me like my husband.*

My mother stayed close to home, learning to fear rather than crave independence. Without the freedom to disagree or feel anger, her sensitivity became the emotional suture for a constantly bleeding family. In doing so, she lost much of the thread holding herself together. She doubted her own instincts and confidence, even though she had a sixth sense of empathy that few recognized as her hidden superpower. Literature professors noticed it and called on her regularly for her insights in class, but in the real world, she felt unmoored.

OCD emerged as an expression of how precarious the world felt to her. It offered her a blameless way of seeking the boundaries and guidance she couldn't ask for directly. When OCD dictates something—when it says, "Please tell me everything is going to be okay, please wash your hands, please help me *right now!*"—it allows for an aggressive urgency that's otherwise forbidden.

This wasn't the full story, only I didn't have words for it then. My mother had so many strengths that I now realize were the upside of OCD—an enveloping warmth that made people feel like their story was the most cherished in the room, a sensitivity to the minute changes of the psyche's secret seismograph, and an ability to enthusiastically decode the most troubling and haunting puzzles within. It followed, naturally, that she became a social worker, and as an apple who didn't fall far from the tree, it was no surprise that I became a psychologist.

But you may wonder, why did I develop OCD if I had the support of a mother who understood this sensitivity all too well? Unfortunately, my mother, the culture, and OCD specialists could not articulate the upsides of OCD. It's why you find me writing here now. As novelist Toni Morrison says: "If there's a book you want to read, but it hasn't been written yet, then you must write it" (quoted in Appelo, 2019).

Like a detective, I tried to unlock the riddle of OCD. For much of my formative years, I thought OCD was nothing more than a problem and sought every method to outwit it. In my graduate school days, I took on specialized training in exposure and response prevention, opening New York City doors with and without tissues, and doing home visits to practice interrupting those persnickety compulsions. I read Freud's classic case on OCD and wrote a dissertation that investigates how to reconcile the conflicted thoughts and feelings surrounding OCD.

Finally, I cracked the code. OCD has hidden gifts and strengths that no one talks about. If we tap into them, we can transform doubts and uncertainty into surprising powers. This is only visible when viewed through the lenses of emotion, metaphor, and relationship.

Like an artist who recognizes the specific names of every color or the musician who recognizes the extraordinary variety of harmonies, with OCD, you are exquisitely tuned-in to feelings and are able to pick up on so much that others simply disregard. Because of this sensibility, you are keenly aware of hurt and heartbreak, and over-rely on your agile mind to make it right. The OCD mind says, "If only I think or do this, everybody will be okay. And just maybe, I'll feel okay too."

It's easy to focus on OCD as a problem. Its behaviors are so dramatic. Yet, its underlying emotions subtle, making them difficult to track. Invisible, like a natural gas leak, these feelings can explode when left unattended. Luckily, you can harness OCD's sensitivity and use it to facilitate greater connection, joy, and meaning.

The goal of this book is to help you notice, name, and claim your secret powers. It's time to talk about what no one ever talks about, and rest assured, it's going to be a joy

THE CREATIVE MAGIC OF BOTH/AND THINKING

Let's *both* reimagine how to use the tools currently out there *and* expand the options for your healing and thriving. To get us started, I'll first highlight what is totally new about the upside approach and share a preview of all the chapters coming ahead. Second, I'll share how the most popular OCD treatments help and why they replaced the older forms.

A little both/and magic, and voila, a new picture of OCD appears. You'll be on your way to the upside.

Both/and thinking (Smith & Lewis, 2022) takes valuable insights from seemingly contradictory viewpoints and finds creative solutions that incorporate aspects of each to solve difficult problems. We'll draw on both/and thinking to conjure the unique magic found in OCD. With it at our side, we'll rescue the dazzling creativity and joy trapped inside you waiting to be freed and shared with the world.

NEW OCD TAKEAWAYS

OCD is a sensibility of sensitivity (chapter 2). You have a very generous heart. As a person with OCD, you are extremely empathetic and tuned-in to the feelings of others. Unfortunately, you regularly push your own feelings and intuitions aside because you're compelled to respond to what's around you first. Then, you get lost in your worried mind. Navigating a new balance with a little "selfish empathy"—as one of my OCD clients affectionately calls it—gets you back to the upside.

OCD carries creative power (chapter 3). You have an expansive mind that runs away with itself and takes you down unproductive rabbit holes, but with help, it can bring on virtuous circles of imaginative possibility. Once we've made the connection—once we have learned how to harness and nurture that unique sensibility—there's so much good stuff that comes from what we've been taught to see as merely a problem.

OCD is working for you behind the scenes (chapter 4). OCD does your dirty work. In its own indirect and strange way, OCD tries to establish boundaries, help you better navigate relationships, and honor your agency and power. When you get to the upside, you will be able to directly take on this creative work without the unwelcome "help" of OCD.

OCD is a wise, wild messenger (chapter 5). OCD reveals, in an exaggerated way, something you're missing. An instinct about feelings you're not fully registering, new information about a situation or relationship, or a hint that you haven't articulated an inner conflict or ambivalence. OCD will *distract* the hell out of you, but it's also trying to *focus* you.

OCD is a unique blend of nature and nurture (chapter 6 and 7). OCD starts with a natural temperament of empathic sensitivity. Without proper environmental support—or worse yet, with environmental abuse or neglect, that is, minimization, criticism, and devaluation—it degenerates into full-blown OCD. Happily, we'll work both nature and nurture to get back to the upside of OCD.

UPSIDE MAGIC: STRATEGIES TO TRANSFORM YOUR OCD

Instead of having OCD rituals and spells, you're going to learn to use your own special magic to use OCD to your advantage and understand what it's trying to tell you, so you don't get caught in its troublesome spirals. Think of yourself as Harry Potter learning how to master a series of spells that you can use in countless scenarios. With the assistance of special exercises, reminders, and tips provided within each chapter, you will learn upside magic to transform your OCD.

THE MOST POPULAR OCD TREATMENTS

The ideas and strategies presented in this book will work surprisingly well alongside the most popular treatments for OCD: cognitive behavioral therapy (CBT) and acceptance and commitment therapy (ACT). But they will also diverge in important ways that are designed to help you up your game in confronting your OCD.

First, let's make sure we have a grasp of the two most common treatments. As they say in the art world, first you learn from the masters and then you go your own way.

EXPOSURE AND RESPONSE PREVENTION IN A NUTSHELL

The most effective and celebrated treatment in the field of OCD is exposure and response prevention (ERP). ERP focuses on the full-blown anxiety that occurs from OCD flare-ups and explosions. The basic idea is that through exposure to your given fear—for example, touching contaminated doorknobs, engaging blasphemous thoughts, or entertaining the anxiety that your partner might not be your soulmate—followed by the prevention of a compulsive response—for example, not washing your hands, not canceling your blasphemous thought with a prayer, or not going through an exhaustive inventory of your partner's greatest hits in love—you can desensitize yourself to that fear.

ERP's most recent advance is "inhibitory learning," which is founded on the idea that you can't unlearn or erase your original OCD fear *completely* but, instead, can create new, safe meanings and experiences that can become strong enough to *inhibit* the original fear itself (Abramowitz, 2018). This new approach is thought to maximize ERP's success in extinguishing OCD's characteristic anxiety.

ERP Misses Your Underlying Emotions

Unfortunately, ERP doesn't focus on the tinder or fuel that leads to OCD explosions in the first place. Remember the fire I spoke about earlier? Those glowing embers are the important emotions fueling your OCD that go unaddressed by conventional OCD treatments.

ERP teaches you to accept your metaphorical house regularly being set on fire by your OCD thoughts. It encourages you to just let it burn with the belief that the response-prevention part of ERP will eventually cut off your anxiety's oxygen source. It assumes that your brain will learn that there isn't really as much danger as you feared, and it will move on.

Now imagine tapping into the positive energy in those emotional sparks instead of relying on your anxiety running out of its oxygen supply. Picture yourself celebrating those emotions (found within your anxiety) and intentionally building a structure to display them, not burning your own home for god's sake! Dazzling as it's set ablaze, like Burning Man, this new structure would be both a radical act of self-expression and self-acceptance and the calling forth of a bigger community. A vision of light in the darkness of the desert.

You don't have to learn something completely new. All the strategies of ERP still apply, but they have a different focus. When you achieve a healthier and safer contact with the core emotions found in your hidden sensitivity and creativity, there won't be any explosions. Even better, this fire will be readily available for creative magic. That's when you know you've connected to the as-of-yet hidden upside!

EXPOSURE AND RESPONSE
PREVENTION DOWNPLAYS MEANING

I've seen OCD described by ERP practitioners as spam or junk mail that should be immediately discarded rather than opened or reviewed (O'Dunne, 2023b). They say you're better off ignoring the content of your OCD because it's just a lie (Overbaugh, 2023). These well-intentioned ideas miss an important and surprising truth: OCD has hidden wisdom in it.

OCD is both meaningful and meaningless. In the pages ahead, I will show you how this is possible and how you can tackle both the problems and the possibilities existing within your OCD with greater subtlety and nuance.

Unfortunately, CBT therapists support only one candidate for the treatment of OCD: exposure and response prevention is the clear frontrunner. Talk therapy isn't helpful and only makes OCD worse; its promises can't be trusted. From this vantage point, OCD is just noise— it lacks meaning, poetry, or any upside at all. To think otherwise is to go against the recovery you claim to want.

We can, however, harness the best of behavioral and talk therapies and reconcile their apparent contradictions with both/and thinking. This conceptual shift entails recognizing that OCD presents all the distracting and diverting static (that which lacks meaning) at the same time as it plays its own unique music (that which has meaning).

ACCEPTANCE COMMITMENT THERAPY IN A SMALLER NUTSHELL

Acceptance Commitment Therapy (ACT) helps you become more zen by teaching mindfulness strategies to help you develop more flexibility, composure, and equanimity around your OCD. It keeps you from getting caught in the undertow of your obsessive thoughts and compulsive urges. We're going to do that here, too, but with a slight twist. We're not just going to *accept* whatever you have coming at you, we're going to *understand* it too.

OCD TREATMENT: FROM ALPHA TO OMEGA

CBT and ACT present an alpha approach to OCD treatment. They champion a tough, muscle-your-way-through mindset but do little to notice, embrace, and honor the sensitive sides of your OCD. Recall that the alpha is dominant, extroverted, and vigilant in protecting the group from threats; the omega is the wolf in the pack who calms others in times of conflict and provides relief with moments of play. The omega brings an intuitive feeling and sensitivity to the group, noticing what's not on the alpha's radar. We need both the alpha and omega to truly heal OCD.

As part of the omega corrective to OCD treatment, we're going to look at how OCD symbolizes what is happening internally and interpersonally and decode it to help you negotiate these issues more effectively. We'll also see how OCD exaggerates and distracts you from the fuller task at hand: psychological integration. All of this takes an inner-directed focus with subtlety and sophistication, but you'll see that it's easy to practice once you understand the method.

THE PARABLE OF THE RAFT

You are trapped on one side of the river where the current is too strong to cross. Even Olympic champion swimmer Michael Phelps himself couldn't swim to the other side, which beckons in the distance with its invitation of safety and calm. You check and there is no bridge or passing ferry to bring you safe passage, and so you must traverse it yourself.

You make a raft of anything and everything you can find: leaves, twigs, logs, creepers, whatever you can get your hands on and piece together. On this sturdy raft, you use your arms and legs and all your might to make it to the other side.

The Buddha asks, "What should you now do with your raft? Since it has served you so well, should you carry it on your back on land?" And the monks reply that clinging to it like that wouldn't be wise or sensible.

The Buddha then says, as if solving the riddle, "What if you now lay the raft on the ground and thank it for its service, and recognize that it is no longer of use to you though it once held for you *everything*?" (Batchelor, 2019).

The monks agree with this perspective, and the Buddha concludes: "And so it is with my teachings, they should be a raft for crossing over, but not for clinging to or seizing hold of" (Batchelor, 2019).

A NEW APPROACH TO OCD

Our relationship to OCD and the teachings on OCD are much like that raft. It is of use to help us cross over, but it is important to loosen our grip on the "raft" when it might yield a newer, more integrated way of reaching the safety of the other side—or of relating to and appreciating the full story of you and your OCD.

That said, you don't have to ditch anything you are doing that's working for you. Rather, I'm asking you to cultivate an open mind and heart to what more is possible if you make the small mindset shift found in the Buddha's profound tale.

Another both/and way to view OCD might be new to you. As I said earlier, current OCD treatments view OCD as *only* a bully, a torturer, and a diabolical menace that torpedoes your life. It doesn't feel like a raft, that's for sure!

It's understandable why this perspective is so popular: OCD harasses, doubts, and nags at you, it doesn't seem like any friend I'd like to hang out with regularly. But the upside of your OCD—the messenger—is trying to protect you, but unfortunately, it ends up persecuting you too, a painful truth that is highly common in many forms of trauma.

Just as ERP encourages us to embrace the uncertainty and ambiguity of our doubts in a behavioral exercise, we can embrace the anxiety of being both right and wrong in our understanding of OCD too. Like a scientist or artist ever ready for a new breakthrough, it's best to cultivate curiosity and fascination with the surprising ways we are often right *and* wrong about our OCD.

Just think, light is *both* a particle *and* a wave! This seeming contradiction opens different ways for physicists to understand and study light. So too, with your OCD. We're going to look at both forms of OCD: the negative (enemy and bully) and the positive (friend and messenger).

We'll see OCD wearing out its welcome as a protective structure. What might have been initially adaptive starts to regularly harass you. A message trying to help you create more boundaries becomes extreme and over-the-top, now making you feel that anything you touch is contaminated. The raft doesn't only save your life but, rather, it pokes and bruises you with its misshapen pieces too.

However, if you give the raft credit for helping you in this emergency and then take proper care to heal your wounds on the other side, there's new territory ahead to discover. On the side of safety, calmness, and enlightenment, as the Buddha implied, you've arrived on the upside. Carrying *yourself* forward—*not carrying the raft*— has been the mission all along.

There's lots of creative magic in the paradoxes of both/and thinking! Sometimes, this process will be counterintuitive, but we are going to hold both sides of what OCD is so that you can reclaim your natural creativity, connection, and happiness. Don't worry if, right now, you can't see OCD as anything more than an awful destroyer of all that you wish to have in your life. We'll make sure to get that negative stuff taken care of to get to the upside.

WHY DON'T CURRENT TREATMENT INCORPORATE THE UPSIDE?

Psychotherapy's study of OCD began in the late 1800s and early 1900s when psychotherapy was a field in its toddlerhood. Freud's seminal case of "The Ratman" (Paul L.) in 1909 viewed OCD through the lens of psychodynamic theory and saw meaning everywhere. Becoming almost obsessional itself, the meaning in Freud's work focused almost exclusively on the potentially sexual and aggressive meanings lurking in one's OCD symptoms. Does the famous obsession with a rat torturing his father and girlfriend represent Paul's erotic desires, his aggressively oedipal striving with his father, or something of both?

OCD requires decoding meaning and finding the hidden, taboo music that comprises it. Treatment for OCD, in Freud's time, explored the imaginative possibilities the symptoms of OCD were attempting to communicate as a messenger. Most importantly, OCD was regarded as a condition caused by hidden, conflicted feelings, not just by nonsensical thoughts.

Over the years, as this focus didn't yield effective results, the radical behaviorists and, later, the cognitive behaviorists took over the OCD field. Their essential take was there is no meaning in OCD; it is only noise. The job of the therapist was to help OCD clients confront their noise and learn how to habituate to it (and drown it out) so they could lead more productive lives. CBT worked by helping people with OCD adapt better to reality and recognize that there was no true threat. OCD, instead, is an unwarranted overreaction—a defective oversensitivity—that can be reconditioned and reprogrammed.

Unfortunately, if you remove meaning from OCD, you also take away the hidden music and poetry within it. It becomes nothing more than static preventing you from enjoying the programming you really want to hear.

Is there any way to reconcile these approaches? How can your OCD be both an enemy and a friend? How can it be both meaningless and meaningful? We'll turn now to a new and old approach for an answer.

INTERNAL FAMILY SYSTEMS
AND RELATIONAL APPROACHES

Both internal family systems (IFS) (Schwartz & Sweezy, 2019) and relational psychoanalysis (Bromberg, 2013; Stern, 2009) recognize an important truth: befriending your feelings, especially those that have been deemed unimportant and exiled, is the surest path to the upside of OCD. Not only will it heal your symptoms, but it will also give you a more grounded, compassionate, and mindful approach to being with all the sides of yourself. Finally, in contrast to CBT and ACT, it will provide the meaning and coherence that so many with OCD realize they've been missing.

Multiplicity (Bromberg, 2013), mindsight (Siegel, 2010), internal family systems (Schwartz & Sweezy, 2019)—there have been many names given to it, but here's how it works. We are each built with sides of self, called self-states, that come with their own stories, feelings, meanings, logic, and motivations. These parts of self make up the integrated self, allowing us to have flexibility, creativity, and range. Despite their contradictions and ambivalences, these stories give us dimension, nuance, and complexity; when embraced, we learn how to regularly inhabit our full humanity.

Psychologist and author Susan David (2018) has an extraordinarily practical and poetic concept that is of great help in making room for your multiplicity. Called emotional agility, it is the practice of befriending and making space for all your emotions, especially your so-called negative emotions, like anger, sadness, guilt, or shame—and allowing them to inform you so you can be more connected, productive, and fulfilled. By changing the way you view these exiled sides, you creatively transform not only your experience but also the way the various sides of yourself interact to create a greater whole. You start to feel more at peace with following the flow and process of your emotions, and you build greater tolerance and openness to what used to feel only like a strain. This is where you'll find the upside.

BRINGING IT ALL TOGETHER WITH THE SPOTLIGHT METAPHOR

Sarah felt like a camera whose aperture opened to take in a greater depth of field than others in her life. "Why do I have to close down my aperture for you? Why can't you see the light too?"

Sarah told me how challenging her ability to pick up on all the feelings of her family, friends, and even coworkers had become. People typecasted her as too sensitive and said she was overreacting. She was told that she needn't get so distracted by what was on the periphery and, instead, should adjust and be like everyone else. Sarah knew better, but she didn't have words; instead, she had OCD.

To bring together all the treatments above and to answer Sarah's questions, we'll use a popular image within OCD treatment: the spotlight metaphor. This metaphor envisions the mind's eye as a spotlight and a bookcase as potential thoughts illuminated and examined by the mind's eye. Books on the shelf are grouped from left to right as "desirable fringe thoughts," "desirable interesting thoughts," "everyday thoughts," "undesirable interesting thoughts," and "undesirable fringe thoughts."

The average mind "brightly [illuminates] the books in the center, somewhat illuminating the books to either side of its beam and leaving what may be additional books obscured on both ends of the shelf" (Hershfield & Corboy, 2013). The OCD mind, in contrast, contains a beam that illuminates nearly the entire shelf.

According to the developers of the spotlight metaphor, Hershfield and Corboy (2013), when you learn to not treat every thought with equal importance and intensity, you will become less plagued by OCD. Put another way, you're too bright for your own good, which becomes a problem like it was for Sarah. Or does it?

ONE MORE TIME WITH FEELING

As they say in acting, "let's try that scene again—one more time with feeling." As we reimagine the spotlight metaphor and CBT treatment, let's not forget emotions. Suppose those books represent not just cognitive, imaginative possibilities but emotional and dramatic possibilities too. In that case, you begin to appreciate the range of people with OCD, their profoundly creative minds and generous hearts.

The challenge that conventional treatments pose is that they attempt to solve the problem of the OCD mind and heart by teaching it to constrict and close off itself. Either adapt to having a more "normal mind and heart" or you can't expect to get rid of your OCD and be successful in treatment. While this is certainly understandable, given the pressing desire of most people with OCD to get rid of their "undesirable fringe thoughts," it betrays their full humanity. It loses sight of the full scope of what the OCD mind and heart are capable of.

Those capacities and powers don't have to be lost, even with OCD treatment. You can transform the negative into nuance to keep the full range of yourself alive. This both/and approach enables and empowers individuals with OCD to benefit from your full Shakespearean scope of feeling and thought.

Instead of imagining the spotlight as a fixed object, with the upside approach, you'll learn how to shift the movement and focus of that spotlight without taking away any of its brightness and sweep. There's so much good stuff in this range that can help temper and soften the truly negative and challenging parts of OCD. Best of all, it can be accomplished without dimming the blaze of the OCD spotlight. Why would you ever want to dim that light in the first place?

Moving forward, you'll see a unique distillation and synthesis of all these approaches. This is the more complex (and yet less complicated!) approach you'll use to reclaim your life.

WHAT'S YOUR OCD ORIGIN STORY?

Artist and OCD advocate Cristi López (Alcée, 2023, April 4) once asked me, "What's your OCD origin story?" From that point forward, I couldn't stop thinking about how vital it is to see yourself as the hero of your own OCD story. It's a compassionate way of embracing yourself in the story of your pain and strength. As a both/and mixture, OCD brings with it much suffering and hurt alongside hidden gifts and powers.

Cristi López recalls sleepwalking as a child straight through her own front door. Not long after, she stumbled on the sinister thought: "Oh my God, I didn't know what I was doing. I could've killed my family with a pair of scissors!" This was when her OCD story began.

My story began when I was in third grade, and I was gripped by the fear that my mother would be killed if I didn't follow orders. Author and OCD expert Shala Nicely's story began when, at four years of age, she and her parents were on their way to feed the ducks but, instead, were struck by a car.

Thinking back on your own OCD origin story, when did it begin and what, if anything, prompted it?

1. What was the scene and situation that first triggered your OCD? What were you thinking or feeling?

2. Now, I'd like you to notice any particular sensitivities you might have had at this moment. Were you sensitized to any particular feelings (fear, sadness, anger, hurt, etc.)?

3. Were there any particular triggers for you? Awareness of death? Separation? Physical or emotional messiness? Something else?

4. Now, let's research other OCD origin stories. They could be those of celebrities who have written about this or other people you know with OCD.

5. Write about what you find here about their OCD origin stories and see if you can catch any parallels. For example, "As I write about Cristi's OCD origin story, I realize that I was also very aware of death early in life" or "I noticed when people's feelings were hurt sometimes before others or they, themselves, did."

2

MAPPING THE HEART OF OCD

THE UNIQUE MAGIC IN OCD:
YOUR EMOTIONAL SIXTH SENSE

Susan Cain (2013) champions the power of introverts. Elaine Aron (1996) showcases the range of highly sensitive people (HSP) (Granneman & Sólo, 2023). Isn't it time we claim the unique magic in OCD?

You're probably well aware of where your magic originates. It's the sixth sense of compassion and empathy that makes it easy to deeply feel and imagine the pain and suffering of others. You quickly notice the sadness, fear, or worry in others *right now*. You even have an uncanny capacity to detect feelings from years past too, what's termed intergenerational trauma (Atlas, 2023).

You're so tuned in that you respond as if such feelings and experiences are your very own. You might also over accommodate the feelings of others without realizing it since you're so skilled at tracking them. Without support, this power becomes a burden that makes you feel overly responsible for the welfare of others.

Research confirms this hidden strength. A July 2021 study from Germany (Salazar Kämpf et al., 2021) found that individuals with OCD show higher empathy levels compared to healthy controls. They shared the suffering of others in both their self-reports and in a naturalistic task designed to test empathy in real time. OCD sufferers also reported more distress over this heightened empathy compared to healthy controls.

Another review of studies (Jansen et al., 2020) showed that those with OCD reported being more emotionally responsive and more likely to feel in tune with others in comparison to healthy controls. Such responsiveness is at the heart of what makes therapists so effective, and yet for those with OCD, it is missing one crucial piece: self-compassion and self-advocacy. Let's see how you can master this new skill and flip the script on your OCD.

THREE STRATEGIES TO GET YOU BACK TO THE UPSIDE

To get to the upside, you need three crucial strategies. The first is to identify and validate what's been rendered invisible on your radar screen—that is, your keen emotional awareness. As you'll see in Kate's case, tuning in to your sensitivity and trusting your instincts changes everything. You'll notice the perks and perils of this sensitivity and learn how to maintain your emotional balance.

I'll show how important it is to befriend and integrate your sensitivity through relationships, whether it comes in the form of supportive family, friends, significant others, or therapy. In order to map the heart of OCD, you must move past a conception that views OCD as only within your own mind.

OCD isn't just happening inside you; it's alerting you to thoughts and feelings about what's happening around you. That's your unique sensitivity. Maybe this is why it's so common for OCD sufferers to gravitate toward each other; they understand what it's like to operate on this special wavelength.

The second strategy is to spot the unique sleight of hand OCD regularly performs. In the case of myself and Lucas, you'll see how quickly OCD plays tricks on us while simultaneously showing its hand. Like a magician, OCD both distracts and focuses us; we'll be spotting OCD's tricks and take your power back so you can be the maestro again. There you'll find OCD's hidden wisdom.

The third strategy is to own and celebrate your unique sensitivity and range and to find more ways to use it in service of yourself and others. That's the creativity of the upside.

MAPPING THE HEART OF OCD

"I almost cried when I read your blog about OCD," Kate confessed during our first Zoom meeting. A cinematographer based in Los Angeles, Kate, was quickly losing hope that she'd ever get past severe OCD that only relented when she was on set. "I always thought that I was failing at treatment, not doing it right; like, why aren't I strong enough to just sit through this anxiety? But when I read your work, I felt like treatment was *failing me.*"

Kate always felt there was something more to her OCD but could never find the words. The nearest she came was surprisingly close at hand: in a quote from Blaise Pascal beneath her email signature, which followed every message: "The heart has reasons of which reason knows nothing."

Kate's OCD sensitivity was regularly undermined by her family and even her therapist. Arguably, her greatest strength was sidelined and devalued instead of nurtured and prized. In response to this, like so many OCD sufferers, Kate became cloyingly apologetic. Her incisive explanation for it had a slight cheekiness, though, that I'll never forget: "I can read that everyone around me thinks I'm so flawed that it just makes sense to apologize in advance."

Despite these glimmers of self-confidence, Kate mostly felt unsure, doubtful, and insecure. Her story had an uncanny echo of my own.

"My parents and siblings used to poke fun at me for not letting go of my teddy bear. I carried her everywhere; she was the sensitive heart nowhere to be found in my house. Why couldn't I be fiercer and face my fears and just grow up? Until recently, I felt the same about my OCD treatment."

Kate nearly idolized the OCD specialist who first diagnosed her and regaled her with the promise of exposure and response prevention (ERP). She finally had hope. If he had saved her, why didn't she feel more appreciative? Kate couldn't understand why she felt such guilt and confusion about this.

As we talked together, it became clearer: feeling wasn't on her therapist's radar, and it rankled her. He didn't listen or seem to care about her sensitivity. It was the teddy bear incident all over again.

"What does it matter what your obsessions mean?" he'd shoot back, as if to say, "get with the program, this isn't getting you anywhere."

In conventional OCD treatment, meaning diverts from the mission and offers unhelpful reassurance. While Kate always wanted to craft ever more intricate forms for her feelings, her therapist wished she'd just assertively work on her behavioral goals. Ironically, there was little room for her voice, for all that good fire in her heart.

Kate detected an unspoken ache in her therapist's heart too—how much his identity was tied to one singular truth and how it rattled him to entertain other truths, especially those that examined the heart's delicate reasons. Her perspective pierced a tender spot in him.

Years later, after treatment, when she was Googling his name to find out more about his personal story, she chanced upon a newspaper headline covering the tragic loss of his younger sister in a car accident when he was only five years old. Kate never put those feelings into words—that she could intuit her therapist's tender spot and his defense against it—because, at the time, she had no direct knowledge. Instead, her feelings metastasized into self-doubt, self-recrimination, and shame.

It clocked Kate in the face one Saturday when she recognized her therapist's philosophy in a widely praised meme circulating in the OCD recovery world: "OCD is just sound and fury, signifying nothing."

Borrowed from Macbeth's famous line when the walls are closing in on his murderous exploits and he learns of his wife's death—ironically,

Lady Macbeth with her "out-damned spot!" is one of the most famous contamination OCD cases in literature—Macbeth's phrase is one of horror, lamentation, and hopelessness. The world is a meaningless, obsessional march of tomorrow and tomorrow and tomorrow, a tale told by an idiot (Shakespeare, 2015).

"What is *wrong* with me?" Kate wondered. "If that meme is right, it's no wonder I'm just a failure in treatment and life."

The middle daughter of a highly educated and successful family of Chinese immigrants to California, Kate constantly found herself on the outside. Family members pegged her as unable to let things go—and although they'd never outright say it—weak for not being more extroverted and independent like the rest of the clan. "Even your work is all just fantasy," her mother complained.

Kate's sister had moved out of the parents' house at twenty-five and was now in medical school, setting sights on buying her first home. Her brother, an IT specialist, always seemed able to fix nearly anything. Kate was an anomaly, still living at home with her parents and never quite fitting into the alpha-driven landscape of her family's California dreams.

"Why couldn't she just enjoy the promise of all that beautiful California sunshine?" her father protested. Kate was always adrift in the riptides of her obsessions: what if she forgot the stove was on, burned the house down, and killed everybody's nascent dreams along with it?

"It's like I can never do what the mainstream wishes for me, maybe that's why I've gravitated to indie films so much. It's my only refuge."

"I'd reverse that," I chimed in quickly as Kate's defense attorney. "The mainstream never really witnessed your profound heart. You've always accommodated others—your family, your therapist, the world—but it's come at the price of who you really are. Your sensitivity has always been a part of what's made your vision so clear and full. It's no accident that your OCD largely vanishes when your sensitivity is prized, as it is when you are working on films and the director gives you the go ahead to command what you need to get the right shot."

Kate has always had a whimsical and perceptive eye, and it has shown in her cinematography. She knows which way to angle the camera not just to get the right light or best composition but to evoke something from deep inside her subjects. Her prodigious talent has landed her on projects that most dream of. Being on set has been one of the few places she has felt free from obsessional doubt.

"Because your parents didn't see your sensitivity as a gift, it got housed in your own mind, and you had to protect yourself and them from its power. You sensed so much of what was happening in your environment but there wasn't a place to communicate that. It becomes wild in our own minds, but we need relationships—and art—to tame it."

Together, we joked about how many artists and innovators had OCD and this unique sensitivity and, if lucky, found a place to give it creative form. Greta Thunberg, herself an OCD sufferer, marshals her profound sensitivity to the neglect of an entire planet into fierce advocacy to save us all from extinction. Young adult author and OCD sufferer John Green chronicles teenagers staring down their own cancer diagnoses in *The Fault in Our Stars* (Green, 2014) and writes of Aza Holmes, the greatest young adult character with OCD in American literature, in his novel *Turtles All the Way Down* (Green, 2017).

Like Kate, Aza Holmes seeks her own center. Is she really just a fictional character without any volition of her own? Is the 50 percent of the bacterial microbiome that makes up the human body in control of her? Aza constantly digs her thumbnail into her middle finger to see if she really exists. But no sooner than she finds herself she is lost again, spiraling about the possible infection she has unleashed.

The heart figures prominently in Aza's story too. Her father, a sensitive soul and unrepentant worrywart, mysteriously drops dead of a heart attack while mowing the front lawn. Just as Kate is so aware of killing everybody's dreams in her life, Aza is terrified of yet another loss in her life too.

Kate was accustomed to having her true interests and concerns fall on deaf ears. Her relationship with her therapist and with cognitive behavioral therapy itself echoed her ambivalent relationship to her parents: while she was grateful for having been raised and financially supported by them, they minimized her interests as foolish and viewed her obsessions as just more evidence of her immaturity and self-absorption. Without a clear and secure sense of support from these relationships—her parents or her therapist—Kate relied on her own thoughts and rituals to hold her up.

And yet here was the rub—without a human relationship to temper them, these thoughts quickly became savage and cruel, an echo chamber for her perfectionistic imagination; selflessness was the only cure.

Kate suffered from paralyzing obsessions when out in public places, fearful that the looks of others somehow might cause her to implode. Dubbed emotional contamination OCD, Kate was terrified that close contact with mean, nasty, or selfish individuals might poison her own personality. Triggered on subways, Kate left the New York film scene for California where she had more freedom to drive solo. But Kate never quite understood why her obsessions centered around this particular theme and not something else.

"It doesn't really matter," her old therapist used to say. That's the trap of it. It wants you to give it attention and believe it has meaning so you'll keep on going down the rabbit hole. It's not to be trusted as your friend."

But Kate, ever-so-fascinated by the motivations of the characters she tracked in the movies she made, knew there must be more. Obsessions have a funny way of both distracting and focusing us on the things we most fear and desire for a reason. Kafka's Gregor Samsa (*The Metamorphosis*, Kafka, 2014) doesn't turn into a bug just because he has a tic of the mind, it is because he is sensitive too. He deeply feels the alienation, oppression, and depersonalization of his family life and modern society combined.

We worked on a new kind of ERP, one that dialed down into all of her feelings and associations to her obsessional fears. As we did, Kate became a more sharply drawn character: she was terrified of being intruded upon, judged, and taken over by the needs of others around her. She was afraid of the imperfection of having her own needs.

With her big heart, she was so tuned into the unexpressed fears and desires of everyone else that there wasn't enough room for herself. She sensed the fatigue in her parents, their loneliness for their home country, and their overcompensated worries about surviving. They had no idea that she was feeling for them internally, unconsciously trying to imagine every way she could help control their fate.

She was compelled to avoid any places with too much scrutiny—subways, planes, trains, long car rides—and wisely found the safest place to exist with complete freedom: behind the camera. There she no longer was the stage for all the unexpressed feelings of others, she could now orchestrate them for her own artistic purposes.

I knew Kate was making progress in our treatment one day when she started our session rather abruptly, "I know you might want to talk more about what we only half-completed last week, but I don't want to do that. This is what I need today."

My heart swelled. I loved the grit, fire, and healthy aggression that I knew she needed to have in order to own herself, even if she risked temporarily losing me. When I expressed this, she was a bit dumbfounded, "You mean, it's okay for me to ask this? I'm not screwing up your plan?"

"Kate, it's always puzzled me why Aza Holmes needed to pick at her finger, but only now do I get it. It wasn't just any finger; it was Aza's middle finger. She needed to say a healthy 'fuck you!' to the people she loved—her mother, her best friend, even her own OCD—and trust that she was entitled it. That's what you're doing now, and I love it."

No matter what kind of OCD you have, there's something crucial to learn from Kate's story: keep your emotional sensitivity front and center. Did you catch all the ways Kate's sensitivity and perceptiveness were misunderstood and devalued? Can you see why Kate was rightfully indignant and then sheepishly doubtful?

Her parents and siblings criticized her for her oversensitivity—symbolized by her teddy bear—all the while Kate herself was silently responding to their emotional fragilities. Instead of being praised and appreciated for her emotional intelligence, Kate became the odd girl out.

She detected the emotional phobia of her therapist too, and it was crushing that he couldn't see and nurture her gift either. Without support and understanding, Kate not only doubted her feelings and perceptions, but her OCD claimed her instead. Recall how she avoided the world that could take her away again and how she found herself behind the camera.

Kate's OCD shifted when she reclaimed her power by asserting her need to talk straight from the heart. For the first time, Kate began seeing something strong and interesting inside her OCD, like amethyst crystals spied inside a rock kicked to the side of a trail. She wasn't broken inside, after all.

Best of all, Kate's creativity didn't just shine on set anymore. She could be an actor in her own right and not get caught up in all the dramas around her. Her fears of riding public transportation and being intruded upon by the glares of others largely faded away. She finally found the upside.

WITH GREAT POWER COMES GREAT RESPONSIBILITY

The gift of heightened empathy comes with its own heartache. As Dostoevsky said, "Pain and suffering are always inevitable for a large intelligence and a deep heart" (Dostoevsky, 1993, p. 264). Your keen powers of reading others and absorbing their emotions can take a toll. It can be confusing, exhausting, and lonely to take in all that information. Like Peter Parker's sensitivity to his neighbor Mary Jane's pain at the hands of an abusive father and insensitive boyfriend, not to mention his attunement to the rest of New York's residents as Spider-Man (Raimi, 2002), it's challenging to be burdened with this hidden strength.

In contrast to Kate's case, I'm going to demonstrate what it's like when your special sensitivity is instantly recognized and supported. It's this kind of mentoring for your unique sensibility that keeps you on the upside. Explicit reminders that your emotional sensitivity is a true gift keeps it in check and encourages the wild side you need to take up your own space too. I've broken this mentoring down into three steps that you can take with you anywhere so it's easier to be your own advocate and champion.

1. *Prize your emotional sixth sense.* Instead of tuning in to your thoughts or behavior, remember that feeling comes first!

Notice your quickness to sense the emotions of others, especially the difficult negative emotions like sadness, fear, and anger, and witness it like I did with Kate. Our mission is to value, nurture, and support this sixth sense. You'll know you've gotten stronger at it when you recognize it before your OCD starts to kick in.

During the winter of the pandemic, the basement became a bunker from which my two-and-a-half-year-old son and I could pretend life was going on as usual. One day, we were amid new adventures, him telling me where his pretend tire and bagel stores were located and running around from place to place. While off exploring some boxes by himself, he noticed my emotions shift without me saying a word.

My eyes wandered to my old piano bench, and straight out of the D. H. Lawrence (1913) poem "Piano" I suddenly recalled both the joyful memories of my mother nurturing my playing and my profound sadness that she never had the chance to meet my son. In a nanosecond, my son asked, "Dada, why are you sad?"

I was amazed at how quickly he noticed the shift in my emotional weather and how accurate he was labeling the incoming front. I've always recognized his emotional sixth sense, the same sensitivity both myself and my mother carried.

I knew that if this sensitivity was not recognized, it might easily devolve into OCD. I praised him for how perceptive he was. As if he had just won at bingo, I shared that he was right; for a moment, I was sad, thinking of somebody I missed and loved very much.

Because I recognized, identified, and responded to his emotional sensitivity, my son easily and quickly resumed his own creative play. Even when I thought I needed to explain further that I was fine and that it's okay to miss people you love, he was already back to himself. I was showing him that I recognized his prowess and skill in deeply tracking emotions, joyfully recognizing and rewarding it with love.

Many well-intentioned parents don't know how to best respond to OCD's sensitivity and are rightfully confused since ERP treatment is so cautious about providing reassurance. They've been conditioned to think of OCD as a problem to be managed and not like I view it, as a possibility to be nurtured.

Since there hasn't been an understanding of and label for this new approach, please be compassionate with yourself as a parent, friend, or significant other as you learn to help someone you love who is struggling with OCD.

2. *Catch yourself before you get caught up in others' storms.* Get clarity on what is and is not yours.

By confirming the reality and validity of his sensitivity and his ability to deeply connect, I gave my son the capacity to draw on his powers of profound empathy without having it become a confusing, overwhelming experience for him. Imagine how different it might be if I had told him, "I don't know what you're talking about, buddy. Everything is fine! Let's keep playing," or worse, "There you go being silly again with your worries; that's just nonsense."

Contrary to other OCD approaches, which leave the impact of relationships out of the mix, our new approach seeks to notice how you are affected by your relationships, not just the other way around—how they are negatively affected by you and your OCD! It's crucial to get more sharpness between what is yours and what is others in your environment; unhealthy and dangerous magic thrives in a state of blurriness.

Our mission is to clarify what is and is not yours, so we can get back to a place where your empathy is tempered, and your self-compassion and self-advocacy are strengthened. We'll go into even more depth on healthy boundaries in chapter 4.

3. Track how your feelings morph into doubts and moral judgments. If you or others don't validate such issues, they will quickly degenerate into obsessional doubts and moral judgments like they did with Kate.

Any kind of denial or minimization would lead my son to doubt his own perceptions and become self-critical and guilty for making me feel bad. OCD places moral responsibility for what isn't in our control: *the feelings of others.*

If my son's sensitivity, for example, hadn't been confirmed, he might have continually searched for closure inside himself to make it right. He might have conjured a feeling of worry and fear over his magical capacity to negatively affect me, not realizing that he wasn't the source of my emotion in the first place. He might have felt overly responsible for something that wasn't his but was clearly present. As with Spider-Man, without harnessing his great power, it becomes too much responsibility.

This third step is the final stage before blurriness and doubt start to spread. At this point, it becomes very difficult to extricate yourself from obsessional spirals.

Conventional approaches to OCD only begin to address OCD issues at this late stage of OCD's impact, and it is for this reason that they require so much muscle. These approaches don't identify or examine any of the emotional and relational issues that we spotted in steps 1 and 2. OCD continues to operate and wreak internal havoc without any sense of meaning or purpose. You are left to think that your worries are totally unfounded. You have little clue how to make them vanish with upside magic.

HOW TO FLIP THE SCRIPT ON OCD

OCD catches us by setting up a problem and throwing us off the trail. It's like fifteen minutes into a *Law & Order* episode (Wolf, 1990–) when you think you've got the case solved, but it's really just a dead end.

OCD doubles, triples, and quintillions down, having us pursue the wrong lead, over and over, because there's a hope beyond hope that it will finally yield its secret. But OCD almost always frames the wrong guy.

Remember how I said that OCD can be both meaningless and meaningful at the same time, both an enemy and a friend? This next vignette showcases a health anxiety obsession. The toothache really wasn't my problem as you'll discover. Instead, the feelings in my heart were the real culprit. As you read, notice if you, too, have had situations where OCD lead you off the trail.

About a month or two into the COVID-19 lockdown, I woke up one morning with a haunting obsession. I could feel a toothache just beginning, and my mind was already out in front: What if I need to go to the dentist and they're all closed down? What if I'm forced to suffer with this pain for days, weeks, or—gasp—months on end? What if I luck out with an appointment, catch COVID-19, and spread it to my entire family?

The more my mind spiraled, the more *real* my toothache became. I could feel the tell-tale signs of a cavity brewing: a relentless headache, tension in my jaw, and a woozy feeling of vertigo. Spoiler: I didn't really have a cavity or need a root canal in the end.

It wasn't an unreasonable or outlandish concern. Living just north of New York City, we were close to the epicenter of the COVID-19 outbreak and, on the news, numbers were climbing every day. We'd see stories about perfectly healthy adults in their prime—like Broadway star Nick Cordero (Paulson, 2020)—felled by this as-yet-unknown invader.

In the past, the obsessional spiral would have totally taken me in. I'd investigate every possible doubt and fear until I was so far down the rabbit hole that I didn't know up from down. But with a new understanding of OCD, I remembered to stop and go a little deeper, and connect to my feelings. OCD has a habit of trying to maintain control by keeping us in our worried minds.

OCD has an uncanny way of alerting us to danger and amping it up, *Spinal Tap* style, to 11 (Reiner, 1984). If we can only understand what it's trying to bring as a messenger, we can find our way out. This is how we begin to flip the script.

Slowly, I questioned myself. Wait, was I the perp now? No, don't worry, I began to question myself as I've been trained as a therapist: with kindness, compassion, and curiosity.

Is there something you aren't allowing yourself to feel? I waited a few moments as I let that steep like a good tea and, slowly, I recognized that I had been trying to show calm and optimism for the sake of my two-year-old—*come on new daddy-o, you be cool, so the kid will be cool.* At the same time, there was another side of me that wondered, *what if this lockdown goes on for days, weeks, months, or even years?*

Jackpot! Here were the beginnings of a classic OCD conflict: the kind of ambivalent love and hate that OCD totally thrives on. If you're a fan of internal family systems (IFS) therapy, you'll notice that I began talking to the different parts of myself. One side was trying to be cool and confident while the other side was feeling scared out of his mind. There were some other side feeling things too—cue the next scene.

I kept interviewing myself for any clues. *Dr. Alcée, Do you remember anything else about that day that seemed a little out of the ordinary? Perhaps anything that seemed just a bit different than usual?*

I remembered a moment when I was playing with my son down-stairs, how he had pretended to visit the bagel store and the grocery store in his imagination since we couldn't do it then in real life, and it broke my heart. A fear and sadness that had been far off in the distance had made its way closer to me like an enveloping but strangely welcome summer storm: we were all in this situation together, but there was a part of me that felt powerless. I was afraid, and I didn't want to admit it to myself.

Ironically, by digging down and tapping into that pipeline of feeling, all of a sudden, the obsession lost its hold on me. By getting to the underlying feelings the obsession was signaling, I decoded its message and reconnected more fully with layers upon layers of my emotional experience.

Instead of seeing OCD as a nuisance, I thanked it for alerting me to subtleties I had tried to push aside. I could see my OCD as the unexpected guest from Rumi's famous poem ("The Guest House"): "violently sweeping my house empty of its furniture . . . clearing me out for some new delight . . . a guide from beyond" (Washington, 2006, p. 17).

Surprising as it may seem, this more mindful approach to OCD, seeing it as a helpful friend and messenger, not just an enemy and demon, is what opens everything. Once you learn how to make this link with your OCD, you'll find it a powerful ally and an unexpected superpower.

Notice again OCD's modus operandi. OCD will try to alert you to a realistic concern or feeling but it will do so in an exaggerated way, just like a bad dream. It will ironically try to get you to stay with the sideshow while missing the main event.

Our job is to make the connection to the full picture of what's going on inside, and then have a true choice in what we can do about it. In both/and style, we're doing both ERP and classic talk therapy at the same time. You're facing the fear but you're going more fully into the feelings co-opted by OCD's sinister charm.

So, what is OCD's method so you can catch it *even better and faster?* It tries to displace our feelings and fears onto something seemingly related, but then that distracts us and uses up all our energy instead of giving us traction on what we really need to emotionally focus on. For example, my toothache stood in for my fears about the pandemic and the sadness, grief, worry, powerlessness, and doubt it was causing. The obsession was close to the emotional concern—a health-inspired constellation of negative emotions—but it was peripheral.

This is the way OCD catches you. It sets up a problem that *is* there, but it throws you off the trail. The toothache really wasn't my problem after all, though I really should cut down on sweets while we're on the topic.

Like a dream (or really a nightmare!), OCD exaggerates the issue so that you have no way to avoid its high stakes. Remember how seriously I took that toothache issue, and how prepared I was for it to go to Defcon 5!

Because the issue is scrambled up in a dreamlike way in the OCD symptom itself, it's often hard to catch (cue *Law & Order* music, da-dah!). Worse yet, people mistakenly take the OCD literally, when it's actually a messenger trying to help you to integrate a fuller perspective.

Just as dreams often showcase worst-case scenarios to help us more deeply process our fears and prepare for their eventual solutions, obsessions do so too. The obsession above referenced a health issue (toothache in place of pandemic fear) and played it out dramatically (like the beginning of a *Law & Order* episode).

What really solved the issues was recognizing the intense powerlessness I was feeling being in lockdown, the culprit we never really expected—the nice neighbor all along.

OCD finds a clever way to both express and conceal the issue to ourselves. Freud described this as a way we manage the overloading anxiety of such difficult inner conflicts.

The good news is when we start to tease apart these different aspects of OCD, like I did with my toothache fear, we get the fuller message and emotional clearing that helps us get in creative flow again. Our OCD is tuned into the subtleties of our experience, which are amazingly helpful if we learn how to read them.

So yeah, while it might seem like the culprit, again, it just may be the unexpected guest who is a "guide from beyond" (Washington, 2006, p. 17).

CATCHING OCD'S SLEIGHT OF HAND

OCD loves to take us down when we're doing well and at our best. Such was the case for Lucas. At the height of his college career, a successful engineering student at MIT, Lucas had just completed his summer internship studying rocket science at NASA. With a group of good friends as he'd always dreamed of having, Lucas was finally feeling confident in his social skin, and then one day, out of the blue, an obsession hit.

Lucas was convinced he was a psychopath. Any violent thought—even minor ones like the urge to swat at a fly—confirmed this new revelation. It didn't matter if he rationally talked it out—a person who worries that he is a psychopath *and* cares about the welfare of others can't *really* be one—Lucas was still tormented by this core and inescapable truth. It was only a matter of time before people found out his true identity, and Lucas lived in secret agony. He couldn't talk about this shameful fear for if he did, it would make it even worse. He was trapped. From this point forward, obsessions sporadically flared up without any seeming trigger.

OCD is like a magician's sleight of hand. It distracts you from seeing what is actually important but look close enough and you'll catch that valuable piece you need for fuller psychological integration. This is what we did in order to get Lucas back after he recalled the college days when his OCD first appeared.

A bit of background first. Lucas was keenly aware of the emotions of others when he was conversing. He tracked the unexpressed fear, doubt, conflict, sadness, and anger like an air-traffic controller monitoring dozens of planes ready for takeoff. He hardly had any mental space to track the path of his own thoughts and feelings, and often found himself flummoxed as to why he couldn't express himself or feel confident. Because he was seemingly so naturally extroverted and analytical—he definitely thought like an engineer—many of his friends and even he didn't recognize this particular emotional sensitivity as any sort of useful intelligence. Most of the time, it felt more like a nuisance than a help.

Lucas was so scrupulous about anticipating what others needed that before he took on a summer job as a salesman, he learned everything he possibly could about every product before he even got trained. A victim of his own success, Lucas was so *good* at all of these things, his psyche needed some way to allow him to be bad.

In this particular session, years after his first bout of OCD, Lucas was now officially entering the workforce and his overactive mind was anticipating everything again. Even at orientation, he felt he should know what to do and say, and if he didn't, who was he? Would he let his family down if he couldn't hack this new job? Was he really just that psychopath waiting to be exposed?

The sleight of hand was occurring right in front of our eyes, but it was so subtle Lucas constantly missed it. Overwhelmed and hopeless, OCD was ruining his life again. Near tears, he wondered how he had reached such a high point only to be felled yet again! He felt it was all over just like when his OCD first started.

Here's where I helped Lucas decode the magic trick of OCD. His OCD was trying to allow Lucas room to be and *feel* bad, only it exaggerated that in the form of the worst thing he could imagine—being a psychopath. Counterbalancing his perfectionistic and overinflated desire to be in total control of taking care of others, the obsession was trying to humble him, not just to torture him but so that he might get the message: he was entitled to have his own needs too. When he suppressed this healthy self-interest, his obsession about being a psychopath emerged in full force.

Lucas's obsession was hiding his profound ambivalence about wanting to do a great job and be a good son to his family and, on the other hand, feeling in over his head and struggling. His main concern was that needing more help might take others down too. When I showed him in session that I could be there to hold him up and that I wouldn't get felled by his obsession too, and that in fact, it wasn't really the *real* message but a scrambled one, the ferocious hold of the obsession loosened.

What were the lessons of this? OCD is an attempt to represent and often exaggerate a hidden conflict, fear, and desire all at once. It creates a sideshow that has some link to the main event, but it is our job to make the connection. Lucas initially thought the main event was making sure he wasn't a psychopath. As we did our emotional detective work, we found it more important for Lucas to allow himself some room to have his own imperfect needs for support, to make room for his fears and guilt regarding imposing on others, and to be more humane with himself about not being totally in control. His black-and-white thinking was leading him to label this healthy need as criminal, as pictured by the obsession itself.

Decoding this is a meaning-driven task, but surprisingly, it provides a much deeper and more profound exposure to your OCD anxieties. While ERP often focuses on superficial layers and levels of your OCD, our new approach taps into the source of fears, hopes, and desires mixed into your OCD. In short, it does more than just resolve your fear, it opens you to the greater range and nuance in your thoughts and feelings.

JOSEPH'S SENSITIVITY OF MANY COLORS

Joseph was puzzled as to why his OCD started. But he distinctly remembered the onslaught of worries about his mother dying he had as an eight-year-old much like how my own OCD fears started. They would haunt him mostly at night while he attempted to sleep only a few towns away from her at his newly divorced father's house. When Joseph described his father to me, it immediately became clear what his obsessions were trying to say.

Joseph's father was a decent, intelligent, and straightforward man, but he didn't have an intuitive or sensitive bone in his body. It's not that he was heartless, he just didn't respond or even perceive the emotional energy swirling around the room, not to mention the stirrings of the heart of a young sensitive boy like Joseph.

When Joseph stayed with his father, he felt alone in the woods without any shelter, like he was the only one who noticed the subtle movements and energy shifts of the night forest and was left to fend for himself if any danger snuck up on him. Comparatively, at his mother's house, Joseph felt safe and warm, as if he were in a cozy brick house seated across from a convivial fire.

Joseph confided in me that though he never quite said it, he always felt that his father would not have truly understood him if he had become too emotional or needy. Always on edge while at his father's house, it baffled Joseph when the strange obsessions about his mother started to take hold.

As we talked about it, I pointed out that some part of him always remembered that his mother was more sensitive and available and could read, decode, and help him contain and express his multicolored feelings. In fact, I told him that whenever I thought of him, I was pleasantly reminded of the biblical Joseph and his coat of many colors (Coogan et al., 2018).

Joseph, too, had access to the manifold colors of emotion, and his father, like Joseph's brothers in the biblical story, couldn't understand him. There were times, Joseph acknowledged, when he secretly wondered if his father was envious of his capacities to see the colors of emotion so keenly, and if he, too, might one day be thrown into a pit because of his own visions and dreams.

"But why would I worry about my mother dying?" Joseph asked.

Because your psyche knew that your mother was the one precious hope you had of maintaining your stability, and without her, you started to worry about the worst-case scenario: she might be dead. Your psyche was wise to notice the difference between what your father and mother could provide in terms of your sensitivity, and you were understandably scared, when you felt alone in the woods, un-companioned with your deep sensitivity.

"But why did I then start to worry that I might kill her?"

"That is very interesting, isn't it? The psyche is funny. It's as if it wants you to be self-sufficient in the ways you wish for, surviving in those metaphorical woods alone. It forces you in this twisted way to have that but then it possesses you. So, you want to be self-sufficient? I'm going to find a way for you to be—I'll take away your mother! It's sinister, but strangely wise in its wish to have you integrate something inside you, but then, it tortures you."

That's where I jumped in to help Joseph realize that he doesn't have to deal with his wonderful sensitivity alone anymore. Nor must he force self-sufficiency in such an over-the-top way, the unwelcome "help" of his obsessions. Being kind and appreciative of this sensitivity, and better aware of how it works, he can now integrate it as a strength rather than as a deficit.

Like the biblical Joseph, and the Joseph I just introduced, though your OCD has kept you imprisoned, you can now become your own royal advisor and trust in the power of your own sensitivity.

UPSIDE MAGIC: NEW STRATEGIES TO FLIP THE SCRIPT ON OCD

Strategy 1. Reclaiming OCD's Hidden Power: Own Your Emotional Sensitivity

Now that you can shine a light on the hidden power in OCD, let's start to keep track of how this emotional sensitivity comes out for you and how you can own it rather than have it own you.

- Are you quick to notice sadness, anger, conflict, fear, or any other such combination of feelings in yourself or in others?
- Which case from above do you relate to most and why? Kate? Lucas? Joseph?
- Have others ever overtly or covertly criticized you for this sensitivity? Have you been self-critical about this sensitivity?
- If you could be an advocate and spokesperson for that sensitivity, what might you say to the sides of yourself (or even others) who are quick to dismiss it?
- How can you reframe the value and power in your sensitivity like I did with Kate, Lucas, and Joseph?

Strategy 2. Focusing on Feelings Sets You Free: Befriend Your Exiles

As someone with OCD, you are quick to use your mind to control your world and the unruly sides of yourself. It's likely the first place you go to make sense of your feelings and to find safety. Yet as much as it tries to help, your overactive mind quickly runs away with itself, bringing on vicious spirals of worry, doubt, and fear. All of it jumbles together to form *anxiety*.

The OCD mind thinks it knows better than the feelings you carry in your own body. It tries to speak for your feelings, but much gets lost in translation. As the old Italian expression goes: *traduttore, traditore*. To translate is to betray. Your mind is quick to believe it is the best messenger, but it so often lacks the nuance of what your feelings can say in their own native tongue.

Let's practice noticing and translating your feelings when your mind tries to speak for them. This can reduce your obsessional spirals and more fully connect you to your emotions and yourself.

BURNING DOWN THE HOUSE

If anxiety is the inferno, feelings are the sparks. It's excellent preventive work to notice the feelings before they start a blaze. Anxiety moves fast and is difficult to extinguish when it's a five-alarm fire. Happily, the feelings underneath are much easier to work with to keep your OCD from burning your metaphorical house down.

To apply this to your own situation, let's use Adam's case to demonstrate how to find your way to your feelings when your mind tries to keep you locked in your obsessions.

HOW TO MOVE FROM ANXIETY TO FEELING

Adam had obsessive worries about his wife's health. He was consistently triggered with obsessive-compulsive anxiety when she ate junk food or large portions of fatty foods—or even worse, when she had too much to drink or occasionally smoked. What from the outside might look like anxiety and controlling behavior was an emotional mix that Adam had largely avoided: fear, anger, and desire.

Now it's your turn. What is the prominent obsession that is fueling your current OCD spiral? Like Adam, what triggers your anxiety the most?

Identify all the emotions within your anxiety.

What are some of the feelings that may be within your anxiety (i.e., anger, fear, envy, sadness, or any other emotion you can identify)? If you are able to identify any, as Adam does above, say or write out any of the particulars about how you feel about the situation.

Identify past sources of your anxiety.

It wasn't totally surprising that Adam had these obsessions. His mother was a lifelong smoker who had died young of emphysema despite so many people begging her to quit. Adam could remember feeling an angry desire as a child to swat the cigarettes out of her hand, as well as the haunting nightmares he had about losing her. He loved his mother very much and had difficulty holding the ambivalence of such strong hateful and loving feelings.

Are there any past sources of anxiety that provide further context so you can be more mindful and compassionate with your feelings?

GOING FOR THE EASIEST AVAILABLE FEELINGS FIRST

Which feeling should you focus on in the mix? Sometimes, it's easiest to go to the least dangerous feelings like desire, love, or even fear.

Adam could talk very openly about how much he cared for and loved spending time with his wife and how much he wanted to live to old age with her. He could also easily talk about his fears of losing her.

Anger is an emotion that OCD therapists often have to model as something okay to explore, noting that it doesn't negate the love or the fear, and also won't destroy the person that is so loved. Adam allowed himself little room to feel anger out of concern that it wasn't fair or would hurt his wife or mother. Why add any more negativity to the mix? But by focusing on each of the component feelings that led to the bigger anxiety, we could better tame Adam's OCD.

Identifying, processing, and organizing Adam's feelings was enormously helpful. Why?

- Up until this exercise, Adam hadn't noticed how much he had been avoiding his feelings and focusing almost exclusively on his thoughts. It wasn't his fault; that's how most OCD treatments are currently structured.

- Having a practical and concrete tool to help him sort through his feelings greatly improved his feelings of self-efficacy, providing him with a much better alternative to the ways his anxiety attempted to maintain control.

- For most people, it's strange and difficult to totally ignore the signals that are coming from inside and trust that they have no inherent meaning or purpose. The exercise provided a more personal and coherent sense of meaning to his particular obsessions and compulsions. It answered why these issues were troubling him so much.

• Adam came away from this exercise feeling that he had a strength instead of a problem. As a result of tracking his quite nuanced emotional experience, he felt proud of the richness with which he viewed himself and his relationships.

WHAT ARE THE FEELINGS UNDERLYING YOUR OCD ANXIETY?

The emotional theme of nearly every form of OCD (harm OCD, contamination OCD, relationship OCD, etc.) is the loss of something or somebody important and precious to you. The rest of the feelings inside your OCD can run the gamut, and we'll focus on a few.

Let's locate the desire first. What do you most wish to maintain and keep in the situation or relationship that is triggering your OCD? Notice how it might connect to other important relationships/issues from the past, as Adam did with the connection of his fears about his wife and his early childhood fears of losing his mother.

What are the specific fears you have about losing a certain person or thing and, by extension, a part of yourself? Notice how it connects to important values and attributes you want to carry inside yourself.

Is there any anger that you have a hard time giving yourself permission to express to yourself or others? Acknowledge that you are entitled to your feelings. Notice why it angers you that this person or situation makes you upset, even if you feel positively about them/it in other ways as well.

Notice whether untangling these feelings allows you to feel more connected to yourself. You might feel a little less chaos in your head or less tension in your neck, shoulders, or throughout your body. Notice how different that feels from being taken over by the anxiety fueling your obsessions and compulsions.

Good! That's the new creative way to approach your OCD to get to the core emotions so you can feel better, calmer, and more powerful.

Strategy 3. OCD Distracts While It Focuses: Guides from Beyond

Remember how Lucas's obsession with being a psychopath was trying to distract him from his own success and power. In what ways might your OCD be trying to distract you?

Lucas's OCD was also trying to guide him to integrate his own badness with more compassion and discernment.

In what ways might your OCD be trying to guide you to something valuable about yourself?

Are there certain situations, when you're at your best or feeling strong, that OCD seems to like to interfere? What are some of those situations so you can be on the lookout?

3

ALL THIS GOOD INSIDE

Masterminding OCD

When the teacher showed the class a film about plastic polluting the ocean and polar bears starving, the girl cried throughout. Some classmates seemed affected but moved on quickly; the girl, however, kept replaying the images in her mind. Saddened and frightened, she couldn't stop thinking about all the what-ifs that the documentary asked. What if this keeps going and we destroy everything on this fragile, spinning globe?

It wasn't long before these same what-if questions transformed into a hopeful one: What if we can do more? That's my question for this chapter: What if we can do more to respond to what's hitting deep into that heart of OCD? What if we can transform the what-ifs of your imagination running wild and recover all this good inside? What if it's possible to face all the scary I-don't-knows that haunt you with uncertainty and take leaps of faith to embrace something bigger?

Many people know of Greta Thunberg's climate advocacy and/or her autism diagnosis, but many are surprised by her OCD diagnosis (Brady, 2019; Farmer, 2019; Gil, 2019). We're not trained to spot the profound sensitivity and depth of feeling that comes with OCD, nor are we tuned into its imaginative power. Thunberg is a captivating example of how it's possible to transform OCD what-ifs into creative why-nots. As George Bernand Shaw—and Robert Kennedy—once said, "Some men see things as they are and ask why? I dream of things that never were and say why not?"

It's not easy to arrive at this new place. Reflecting on her own journey, OCD advocate Catherine Benfield (OCD Action, 2022) spies a powerful truth: "Everything that happened in my life had a kind of what-if attached to it. I've always had a really incredible—I see it as incredible now. At the time, it was more of a curse—imagination." This imagination is interrupted by the curse of what-ifs constantly raining down until, one day, you notice the flowers and take hold of their beauty. Then, you start asking a new question: *What If I can be and do more?*

This chapter is going to showcase all the good you have inside (the combination of your generous heart and imaginative mind) and how to tap into it, transforming your thought spirals into virtuous circles. You will learn how easy it is to get to the *nuanced* from the *negative*, and why it's been so difficult to make that shift. You will mastermind your OCD.

This good inside is more sophisticated and powerful than you may have realized. If you're reading this book, you may not have received the support needed for a fuller conversation with this inner richness and complexity. Until you make the "good inside" shift, OCD steals your creativity and depletes your energy. Like having too many apps running on your phone or computer, there's less working memory for you to access and run other programs. You regularly crash and shut down.

GETTING TRAPPED IN YOUR OWN WHAT-IFS

You're probably very familiar with OCD's what-ifs; the list has infinite variety. Benfield's what-ifs as a child revolved around washing, checking switches, and looking out windows to make sure people were coming home safely. After the birth of her son, intrusive what-if thoughts started off with the possibility of her cat sitting on him, moved on to the potentiality of others accidentally hurting him, and then, naturally, arrived at her worst fear: the likelihood of herself as perpetrator harming him. Her what-if thoughts also centered around reviewing the past for her goodness as a mother.

OCD quickly jumps in, giving you a way out of your what-ifs with "if-then magic," but the "blessing" slowly (and surely) becomes a curse. As OCD advocate Joe Alterman (2016) notes:

> To me, I've always looked at OCD as if I don't do this, then this is going to happen. If I don't do a bunch of things, my parents are going to die while they're out. Or there were certain people at school who I didn't like, I thought they were jerks. I remember, if I don't do a certain amount of things, I'll become just like them.

THE MAGIC INSIDE YOUR WHAT-IFS

Good news! Creativity and magic are close at hand. Research supports this, showing that OCD is highly correlated with a number of everyday creative activities including writing a short story, making up a joke, writing a poem, making a sculpture, or redecorating a room. In a recent study (Furnham et al., 2013), OCD accounted for 32 percent of the variance in creativity; in other words, OCD is a key driver of your creativity in many areas but has been waiting for you to link it up with the rest of yourself.

We've already seen a preview of the what-ifs that try to take you away from the good inside. From Kate denying the goodness of her sensitivity to Lucas assuming he was a closeted psychopath and my own fears about a toothache, these what-ifs take us out. Fortunately, it's possible to transform them and find your way back to the upside.

THE PERILS AND PERKS OF AN IMAGINATIVE MIND

People with OCD are incredibly creative and have constant curiosity, always seeking answers to "what-ifs?" Right now, this seems like an awful thing because it is misused to torture you. As writer Elizabeth Gilbert (2016) notes: "Possessing a creative mind, after all, is something like having a border collie for a pet: it needs to work, or else it will cause you an outrageous amount of trouble" (p. 171).

Not many have given your OCD mind the herding work it craves, the purposeful order it seeks. Instead, it runs back and forth inside you with: What if I didn't lock the door? What if I thought something cruel? What If I don't really love my partner?

The what-ifs fueling OCD anxiety are connected to an addiction to certainty: I must know and anticipate all contingencies in order to be safe (Schwartz, 2017; Rockwell-Evans, 2023). I will doubt myself and the world until I get absolute and total assurance. We need to borrow a rebel's attitude to temper these fears.

FROM WHAT-IFS TO WHY-NOTS: THE CREATIVE POWER OF UNCERTAINTY

In both science and the arts, innovation and discovery come from courting possibility, allowing space for your I-don't-knows to commingle with wonder and delight (Szymborska et al., 2000). This perspective doesn't demand perfection or certainty but instead relishes the emergence and unfolding of a creative process. It embraces the playful, dreamlike, and metaphorical freedom to be one thing and then another without smoothing over contradictions. It comes from trusting in a bigger picture and allowing yourself to be a little bit of a rebel.

OCD what-ifs, in contrast, plummet you down rabbit holes of doubt, rumination, and *fear*. This is "creativity used to make us miserable," OCD expert Jonathan Grayson (2020) says, the kind governed by fear, anxiety, and criticism. With a few important strategies, it's possible to transform the what-ifs into a muse rather than a critic.

I'll show you how to transform the negatives of your what-ifs into the nuance of "what more can I be and do," helping you gain full access to the richness of your feelings and thoughts and all of the sides of yourself. You'll learn how necessary it is to try on that rebel, practicing being a little more brash and bold in face of uncertainty. And finally, you'll take inspiration from others with OCD who have put these practices into action.

As we previewed in the previous chapter, following your feelings brings your wild imagination together with your tender heart. We'll need a dreamlike metaphorical method to make this all possible.

VICIOUS CYCLES AND VIRTUOUS CIRCLES: MOVING FROM NEGATIVITY TO NUANCE

Unfortunately, the majority of people with OCD are most familiar with the dark side of their imagination: when it hijacks their headspace like cancer cells, crowding out any possibility for creative action. Author and OCD sufferer John Green (2018) describes a typical thought spiral as follows. While eating a salad, it immediately occurs to him that someone might have bled into it and now he is unable to move on to another thought, with the obsessional what-ifs continually expanding. Thought spirals like this are the opposite of meaning, order, and inspiration: they are never-ending gaps constantly seeking closure and resolution.

But is there a way to get out of an OCD thought spiral? It so happens that the way out of a thought spiral is connected to the good inside that most people miss within their OCD: *nuance.* OCD expert Jonathan Grayson notes that OCD sufferers view the world with complexity and nuance rather than with simple certainties and absolutes. Many think this only leads to more uncertainty and doubt, but it's actually a strength that gets you back to the upside.

In her studies on the wisdom and wonder of uncertainty, Maggie Jackson (2023) writes: "Our uncertainty is both a signal of possible danger and the state of mind that invokes the considered thinking needed to update a now deficient understanding of the world" (p. xviii). Unfortunately, many with OCD immediately go to the negative instead of allowing emotional and intellectual space for the nuance waiting within them.

OCD sufferer, musician, and record producer Jack Antonoff echoes the importance of sifting through the complex, yet nuanced, emotional baggage that we all have in order to find what is useful and valuable— especially for those with OCD, who notice so much of what's crammed inside. In a *Time* interview (Lansky, 2017), he sums it up best:

> We all have this stuff we carry in an invisible suitcase. You can't keep it all, because if you keep it all, you can't move forward. But you can't let it go, because if you let it all go, you're not yourself. The great balancing act of life is, *What do I keep in here?* (para.1; emphasis added)

In order to properly figure out the answers to those questions, you need to learn what is truly inside your OCD: the good, the bad, the ugly, and everything in between. And it's a bigger process than merely finding relief for symptoms. Again, as Antonoff reflects:

> So there's a scale where it's like—can you leave the house? Can you connect with people? Can you care for yourself right? If you can't do those things, you have to heal. But everything else, I think, is an attempt to understand. I want to understand why I feel certain ways. I want to understand why I can't do certain things and can do other things. I want to get *myself* the way I get *other things*. (Lanksy, 2017, para. 15; emphasis added)

So how do you find that understanding when so much of current OCD treatment says that talk therapy isn't really helpful for your OCD?

NUANCE SAVES THE DAY

Nuance doesn't fit neatly into categories, and so the mind, without assistance from a tender heart or supportive relationships, resorts to extremes. That's where OCD fools you. OCD tricks you with all-or-nothing shortcuts. You feel compelled to be the worst or the best—you have committed the most heinous crime imaginable, or you are immaculately pure. There's little room to engage these heart-rending internal conflicts in a way that's creative and constructive.

Notice how the either/or and black-and-white thinking tries to trap you. It attempts to keep things linear and forgets that the world—and our hearts—work in nonlinear ways too. Remember that light as a particle and a wave we talked about in the previous chapter? Remember how the heart had its own reasons of which reason knew nothing?

Nuance is a funny thing. Derived from the Latin word for clouds, nuance originally referred to their complex shadings and subtleties. In one sense, when something is "cloudy," it means it is difficult to see. Interestingly, the cloud from which the word nuance comes means there is more to see. Nuance captures the subtlety and texture of the world and illuminates it. The word itself is a perfect example of how delightful and challenging it is to hold complexity. Nuance, like the clouds, is everything and nothing all at once. It is wholly insubstantial and yet can shapeshift into the most intricate forms imaginable. Remember as a child discovering what you could make of the clouds? Unfortunately, we stop playing this game. Our minds are quick to oversimplify. We stop noticing the nuance and start favoring the negative.

Moving from the Literal to the Metaphorical: The Surprising Bridge to the Upside

In John Green's (2014) novel, *The Fault in Our Stars*, we see how such a conventional, unimaginative view throws us off track. Fresh out of a cancer support group, teenager Hazel Grace Lancaster is charmed by witty, kind, and handsome Augustus Waters who has just invited her to take a risk and watch a movie with him, a complete stranger, in the middle of the day. Who does that? Even though she playfully protests that he could be an ax murderer, she's also curious and intrigued by how it might unfold.

Suddenly, Augustus pulls a cigarette out of his leather jacket pocket and Hazel is horrified. She jumps to a conclusion that most of us would if we, too, only tuned in to literal, all-or-nothing interpretations. Not only has Augustus completely killed Hazel's intrigue but it's as if he has no idea how devastating—literally devastating—cancer is. Or has he?

Hazel doesn't know the nonlinear and symbolic perspective Augustus has adopted: there's more nuance than meets the eye beyond a simple, literal way of viewing the world. Augustus speaks as if awakening Hazel from a trance: "Hazel Grace, they don't actually hurt you unless you light them. I've never lit one. It's a metaphor, you see. You put the thing that does the killing right between your teeth, but you never give it the power to kill you. A metaphor" (Green, 2014, p. 20).

You might think John Green's literary act is *just* the ultimate ERP (exposure and response prevention) moment: taking the thing you're most afraid of, that's most dangerous, anxiety provoking, and upsetting, and putting it right between your teeth. But I see it as illustrating a novel way to reimagine OCD treatment: What if there's more nuance to how we can see OCD standing there before us like Augustus? What if we've been looking at OCD too literally all along?

Many sufferers and therapists relate to OCD in this literal way: OCD is *only* an affliction, a curse, and a waking nightmare. They fail to see the upside that has its own hidden poetry and can only be accessed using a metaphorical approach.

Losing the Good and Finding It Again: A Biologist Rediscovers Life

There is speculation that Charles Darwin, the renowned scientist, biologist, and naturalist best known for his revolutionary ideas about evolution, had obsessive-compulsive disorder (OCD-UK, 2022a). Darwin struggled with relentless doubts about being properly understood. In one instance, after an innocuous conversation with the Vicar of Downe, he couldn't sleep and returned to the Vicar's house to check that he hadn't conveyed the wrong impression. He was kept awake at night obsessing about little things he had done during the day or about how his children might inherit his own weak constitution, compulsively closing his eyes firmly to try and make the thoughts go away.

Darwin often sought reassurance from others and tried to soothe his own harsh conscience—he was often described as "pathologically modest" and the recognition of even a tiny dose of vanity in himself was a course of distress—with the mantra that he repeated hundreds of times to himself: "I have worked as hard as I could, and no man can do more than this" (OCD-UK, 2022a, para. 5). Despite this, we also know that he channeled his obsessional capacities into revolutionary and nuanced ways of reimagining ourselves. He was a bit of a rebel too.

Our next case, Alexandra, also a biologist, suffers from a similar OCD, prone to completely losing her own center of authority. Nuance brings her back.

Alexandra was excited about a biology research project she was spearheading that was synthesizing totally new insights in her field. When she shared her findings with her mentor, he was suspicious of how she interpreted the data and had a dramatically different take.

Almost immediately, Alexandra spiraled into malignant OCD doubts that her project was a waste of time and she was a failure. All the excitement quickly devolved into a barrage of intrusive thoughts that questioned everything she knew. Like Kafka's character Gregor Samsa in *The Metamorphosis* (Kafka, 2014), Alexandra felt like a bug on its back, struggling to get upright, stuck. She couldn't get out of bed. She was trapped in the never-ending labyrinth of her obsessional mind. Soon enough, she was compulsively searching the internet for ways to reclaim herself. The more she searched, the more lost she became.

Alexandra wasn't allowing room for her heart's reasons and was subconsciously trying to avoid them. Unfortunately, as psychologist

Terry Real (2023) observes, "We human beings cannot be surgical with our feelings. If you open up to one feeling, they all come."

Alexandra turned her what-if's and I-don't-knows into why-nots, creating room for her full feelings, all at once. She allowed herself to feel a strong desire for the approval and support of her mentor and her anger and disappointment in his failure to back her ideas with more encouragement. Alexandra also remembered how quickly and easily she took on other's positions at the expense of her own.

This step enabled her to reclaim her solidity by keeping track of the many different angles of her experience. Alexandra began to empathize with herself again. She could witness the understandable conflict she had about needing and respecting her advisor while also wanting her own voice, irrespective of him. She took on the nuance of the situation—holding everything and nothing all at once—in order to break free of the negative.

As soon as Alexandra made these connections and allowed her inner rebel to talk back to her spiraling OCD, the intrusive thoughts vanished. Even better, now grounded, she had powerful responses to her advisor's critiques and even found creative ways to incorporate them into her own new insights. She took advantage of her receptivity to the complex perspectives of others and creatively integrated them with her own.

Reclaiming the Best of Both Worlds

Instead of losing herself completely or feeling like the world itself was crumbling, Alexandra held on to both. Instead of succumbing to the sadistic, impersonal critic that her OCD was trying to induce, she tapped into the creative power of all the good inside that we've been highlighting.

Emotionally, OCD tries to censor aspects of difficult, often conflicted, feelings and convince us that the solution is to keep tinkering with the OCD sideshow. Recall the tricks and sleights of hand that

OCD played with Lucas, as well as with me and my toothache. Instead, if we lend that big heart of empathy to ourselves instead of using it to just rescue others or save the whole world, we'll find our footing and solidity again.

FLIPPING THE SCRIPT BY EMBRACING THE REVERSE SIDE

Stephen Dunn's poem "The Reverse Side" beautifully illustrates the process of holding on to oneself while being open to new ideas and emotions that advance complexity and mystery. As the speaker tells one seemingly absolute truth, he quickly feels a fool, "as if a deck inside us has been shuffled / and there it is—the opposite / of what we said" (Dunn, 2000, p. 73). So slippery and humbling is this process that he wonders if that is why, as we are falling in love, we are already falling out of it, too.

This is a great description of how OCD makes us feel. One moment, we might be feeling totally fine and self-assured, and the next, it is like our whole sense of the world and our very existence are in question. For those with OCD, there is a quickness to see the problematic, negative, and maddening sides of this openness to multiple perspectives. But Dunn redeems it as a noble and beautiful human gift, all the while commiserating that it isn't easy to maintain our bearings.

Embracing Your Negative Capability

OCD can strike as a cruel and sadistic Kafkaesque torturer, but it can lead us to what poet John Keats calls negative capability: the capacity to accept and embrace the complexities, mysteries, and beauty of what is not fully understood by logic alone. Dunn acknowledges the difficulty and challenge of negative capability, writing "How do we not go crazy / we who have found ourselves compelled / to live with the circle, the ellipsis, the word / not yet written" (Dunn, 2000, p. 73).

This second step of flipping the script on OCD involves cultivating the richness of negative capability. This is an aesthetic and creative extension of the ERP premise of tolerating uncertainty. It re-animates the world and accepts and embraces its beauty, meaning, and order even within the ambiguous moments that throw us off balance.

When we integrate these two sides—an enormously imaginative, active, and roving mind with an open, searching, and tender heart—we flip the script on OCD. Like Dunn's speaker, we find a way to live with the circle and the ellipsis, and, paradoxically, we also find a straight line back to the center of ourselves.

You Must Be Bad, Brash, and Bold

Remember Augustus again, the cancer survivor placing an unlit cigarette between his lips? Like Augustus, you need to be a little brash, bold, and bad to get to this good inside OCD. It's part of why ERP is so appealing and useful for folks with OCD; it gives permission to be bad. But ERP is never fully satisfying. It's missing feeling and imagination: all that good inside.

ERP doesn't help you become more curious about the metaphorical: the underlying feelings, conflicts, and concerns you're tuned into with your exquisite sensitivity to nuance. Being fully human means that you are taking into account feeling, thought, and meaning. Without this holy trinity, life feels unmoored, incomplete, and purposeless. No amount of getting past your rituals will make you feel fulfilled and at peace; an exercise of sheer willpower can't incorporate this bigger picture.

CONTAINING MULTITUDES

Your inner world is a metaphorical place. To get in touch with it, you need to lean into your imagination rather than disconnect from it by becoming too literal. We are each built with sides of self, called self-states, that come with their own stories, feelings, meanings, logic, and motivations.

I like to tell clients that therapy brings all of their different selves to the metaphorical table so that a conversation can be had (Alcée & Sager, 2017). Some selves will talk more, some less, and others might not even be invited or allowed at the table at all. Although these self-states can conflict and antagonize each other, they can also complement each other, providing a whole that's greater than the sum of its parts. Poet Walt Whitman says it best: "Do I contradict myself? Very well, then, I am large. I contain multitudes" (2002, p. 77).

People with OCD are very concerned with making sure their good-me sides stay clearly separated from their bad-me sides, which have to be constantly monitored and, all too often, overregulated. These are the wild sides that need to be tamed, like Max found in *Where the Wild Things Are.* The bad-me parts of self—the violent, aggressive, sexually taboo, morally reprehensible sides—are suppressed and almost get converted into not-me sides of self.

Not-me sides of self are the most shamed, humiliated, and traumatized sides of self. They cannot even be named or spoken about and are only communicated enactments, unconscious attempts to make them visible through relationships. Most of the OCD symptoms people experience—feeling selfish, petty, mean, impulsive, thoughtless, dangerous, or callous—fall into the bad-me category but at times, since they feel so shameful and reprehensible, they blur into the not-me category.

As problematic and distressing as OCD symptoms are, your psyche's attempt to symbolize and represent your inner conflict is a very healthy sign and showcases its effort to keep these issues from being completely dissociated and ignored. Our job is to find ways to bring these sides back into play. Let's see how a painter does just that.

Instead of banishing scissors due to the sharpness and potential aggression and violence they can represent, we'll see how the painter incorporates these aspects of herself in nuanced ways. She invites these sides of self to be humanized and personified—made into image, thought, and feeling—rather than leaving them to swirl around in an impersonal stew of fear, terror, and doubt.

RECLAIMING YOUR SELVES

Scissors feature prominently in artist Cristi López's paintings. She ties this back to her OCD origin story—some of Cristi's earliest memories are that of a deep and unrelenting *fear* that she would accidentally kill her entire family in her sleep.

Cristi was an avid sleepwalker from childhood through her teenage years, and the knowledge that she was capable of unconsciously doing things ignited a fear of her own violent potential that consumed her. As the dysfunctional cycle of OCD took hold, she requested that her parents hide all sharp objects in the house. Obsessions of doing harm trailed her at every turn, and scissors were among the most feared objects.

But just as all superheroes have an origin story, they also have a superpower that is born of it. In her artwork, Cristi turns what is *diabolical*—Greek for what tears us apart—into something *symbolic*—Greek for what brings us together (Kalsched, 1996). She reclaims the metaphorical in her OCD and in doing so liberates and enlarges herself.

"Scissors are a recurring motif, representative of the obsessive violent thoughts that plague many sufferers of OCD. My figures do not shirk from this object and its violent potential as their fears would have them. Rather, they wield the object of their fear, often visibly cut and bleeding. In the context of my work, scissors are a symbol of reclamation," Cristi told me recently as I was interviewing her for her first solo art exhibition.

Instead of torturing herself with a false choice—she is either a good person or a murderer—Cristi has incorporated a more complex, nuanced, and compassionate view that she can be both caring and moral, on the one hand, *and* powerful and fierce, on the other. By befriending rather than suppressing or denying this conflict, she has allowed it to have a dialogue in her art and her life. And notice how, like Augustus in *The Fault in Our Stars* (Green, 2014), Cristi unites the feared object both literally and figuratively.

Cristi's art and life embody this notion of complexity and nuance that we are getting at. Instead of trying to beat the OCD, she joins it and finds ways to give it form and voice. In so doing, Cristi allows her bad-me sides—the exiled sides of her hidden assertiveness, sensitivity, and brashness—to join together with her good-me sides to form the complex portraits she creates. She transforms what could be a vicious cycle into a virtuous circle.

One of Cristi's paintings, titled "Unravel," depicts a wounded female nude against a Chicago skyline backdrop. Like those who suffer and soar due to OCD's hidden sensitivities, the main figure carries power, confidence, and emotional vulnerability; she evokes a sense of duality, intimacy, and frenetic calm. When I asked Cristi about how she learned to integrate her sensitivity and strength, she told me:

> When I was twenty, my therapist encouraged me to try reframing my sensitivity by reading Elaine Aron's *The Highly Sensitive Person*. This was the first time I saw sensitivity painted as a potentially positive, even powerful, trait. I can't count the number of times in my life that my sensitivity has been cited as a problem, an inconvenience, and something to be remedied. The traits I possess that were reinforced and encouraged by the schooling system included *perfectionism*, rigidity, structure . . . things that made me a model student. That's not to say that my creativity was always stifled, but my sensitivity and emotionality weren't celebrated the way that my perfectionism was and certainly not linked to my academic success in the way my discipline was. I think that both structure and creativity are integral to a balanced life, but, aided by the all-or-nothing tendencies of OCD and cultural messaging, I overdeveloped the structured parts of me to the point where I was incapacitated.

In Cristi's artwork as in her advocacy, we see the beautiful, nuanced, and complex integration of all the good inside that forms the upside of OCD.

INTEGRATION AS PSYCHOLOGICAL DEPTH PERCEPTION

Current treatments for OCD—especially cognitive behavioral therapy (CBT) and acceptance commitment therapy (ACT)—focus on OCD as a literal thing. Unfortunately, it's like looking at OCD with only one eye open. We need two eyes on OCD to truly distinguish its depth and dimension. That's our new both/and approach.

CBT and ACT have done an excellent job of focusing, with one eye, on the literal aspects of OCD: targeting what the fear is and *literally* confronting it—licking your hand after touching a dirty doorknob—or *literally* conjuring it—handling a knife around a vulnerable family member. They also do very well at focusing on OCD from a mind-based perspective: these thoughts are just like waves on the ocean, ever changing, but not worth holding on to.

The second eye that I'm referring to, however, focuses on symbolism and emotion. It tracks the feelings that give rise to OCD anxiety, those that stem from the protective, wise, and exiled sides of self that are trying to communicate with you. It's also open to the dreamlike metaphorical ways in which your imaginative creativity can be used in service *of* rather than *against* you. It's not as direct and linear as typical CBT treatments, but it's a more hopeful and complex vision of what OCD is; and I think you'll find it extraordinarily helpful.

This metaphor of two eyes working together to perceive OCD anew and in its more powerful and complete form describes, in the literal sense, how we are actually built. We have a left and right brain that each specialize in complementary functions that combine to create the magic of being fully human. This is our vision for OCD—no pun intended: we need to treat and heal your OCD, and we need to see how much more you can do, not just despite your OCD, but because of the underlying sensitivity, complexity, and empathy it offers.

Using literal approaches like CBT and ACT as the *only* methods of treatment are not enough. Internal family systems and psychodynamic therapy offer a metaphorical corrective. Without them, we can't see the full picture. They help you tap into your imagination in a new way that rediscovers all the good inside.

AN INTERNAL FAMILY SYSTEMS APPROACH TO OCD

Internal family systems (IFS) therapy has become a very useful and powerful complement to current OCD treatments (Schwartz & Sweezy, 2019; OCD Action, 2023). It offers a useful way of labeling the sides of self that are related to good-me, bad-me, and not-me sides that are found in relational psychoanalysis. In IFS, there are no bad parts. All sides of self are valuable in their own right and need their time onstage.

Exiles are the young, traumatized parts of the self that must be protected from what is too much to emotionally bear—the pain, fear, and terror that can't be managed without the support of regulating adults. In the case of OCD, these are the highly sensitive and empathic sides of self that are rarely given proper help and validation; instead of being able to regulate all that they are experiencing, other selves come to the fore to manage on their behalf.

Remember how my son could detect my sadness with his sensitivity? If a child has repeated experiences of their sensitivity being shamed, ignored, or minimized, this part of them will go into hiding. These exiles will be taken care of internally by two different kinds of protectors: the manager and the firefighter. When working well and healthily integrated, the manager negotiates situations and sizes them up so that control can be realistically achieved. When the manager is not integrated, this side of self takes on a downright impossible level of control.

In OCD, you can see the manager most vividly in an overactive mind that perpetually anticipates danger and regularly attempts to manage it by thought alone. At its core, the manager is performing an important function: protecting you from feelings of rejection, hurt, sadness, and terror. The manager cares for the exiled sides of self by keeping them dissociated and separate.

The firefighter comes to the fore when the manager can't do the job and an immediate, all-hands-on-deck response is needed. When a psychological issue is well-integrated, the firefighter uses the body in constructive ways, serving as an emergency response that learns to healthily soothe and comfort, like reminding oneself to take a walk, remember to breathe, or to replenish with a good meal or sleep. But when the firefighter is used in a reactive, unintegrated way, it leads to the quick-fix compulsions so often seen in OCD.

The reactive, unintegrated firefighter says, "If you don't do this compulsion now, everything will be burned!" That healthy fire we've been trying to harness, here, wreaks havoc and causes a five-alarm. The symptoms of OCD are your attempts to represent and negotiate these sides—the exile, the firefighter, the manager, the bad-me, and the not-me—but they take on a life of their own, as if they are no longer part of the self at all and are just possessive and threatening disruptors of the natural order.

The brash and rebellious work I've spoken of comes in with identifying and having more compassion and curiosity about your "bad" sides and learning how to befriend and learn from them rather than exiling or excommunicating them.

LEARNING HOW TO READ THE CHANGES

In jazz music, "reading the changes" refers to the player's capacity to notice and respond to the various harmonic changes happening in the music and being produced by the other musicians, and the capacity to embrace dissonances while making something new out of what seems old and familiar. It is the art of making music out of what seems like nothing more than noise.

Having OCD is like having the capacity to read the changes really well but never having been taught how to put it to use by any real-life mentor. On your own, it's easy to get overwhelmed by notes and harmonies that are so rapid, full, and complex that you can't figure out how to convert the chaos into coherent music. Before you even begin playing, you fear every wrong note you *might* add to the mix, because you haven't been taught how much good stuff you can bring to the jam. Without a ready category for such complexity, it's easy to go straight to the negative. It's not easy to learn how to play the blues.

You don't have to play music in order to "read the changes," but our next OCD advocate is one who can do both. He sees the good, hopeful side of OCD that developed from proper mentoring and, surprisingly, for him, from inspiring words not only found in therapy but also echoed by jazz greats like Sonny Rollins, who once told him: "We all have to use adversity as an opportunity to find a way. So, keep a strong mind throughout this short existence. Your examples give us all hope, as all of us here in this life have to struggle" (Alterman, 2016, para. 34).

Joe Alterman suffered from a variety of OCD ritualizing— needing to write a perfect letter "p" before moving on to other letters in a timed exam (you can imagine how stressful that was!), placing his phone perfectly into his charger at night, washing his hands, smiling into the mirror over and over again, and making sure he pet his dog before sleep or else he didn't truly love him. The list goes on and on, but you get the idea.

For Alterman, these obsessions moved on to ritualizing magic numbers—like three—believing that if he didn't do his xyz-routine correctly, he'd need to repeat it a certain number of times. This OCD ritual echoes that of another OCD sufferer: engineer and inventor Nikola Tesla (OCD-UK, 2022b). With more than seven hundred patents to his name, and best known as the developer of alternating current, Tesla reportedly developed OCD in 1917. On his daily swims at the public pool, Tesla always swam thirty-three laps; however, if his count was interrupted, he had to start over from zero. He frequently had the compulsion to circle a city block three times before entering a building. He also made sure to reside in a hotel room with a number divisible by three, living the final ten years of his life in suite 3327 on the thirty-third floor of the New Yorker Hotel.

So much of what Joe felt forced to do was restricting his sense of what he could feel and show the world—that is, until he found jazz piano. Miraculously, the richness and complexity of jazz enabled Joe to safely put form to his feelings and it "could all pour out." He could play for hours at a time.

This new creative ritual became so important because it allowed him to discover, express, and contain the various shadings of what he thought and felt, and the mentors he had in Sonny Rollins, Ahmad Jamal, and Les McCann demonstrated a way he could appreciate that complexity instead of using it to punish and harm himself. Alterman shows us how we can embrace nuance rather than let ourselves slide into the negative.

WHY DOES THE PAST MATTER ANYWAY?

In a recent blog post, Allison Raskin (2023a) came out hard with this upper cut to the chin: "I'm going to admit something that might get me in hot water with the mental health establishment. I'm not a huge fan of assuming that everything about you can be linked back to your childhood" (2023b, para. 1). Both an OCD sufferer and author of a book on relationship OCD, *Overthinking About You: Navigating Romantic Relationships When You Have Anxiety, OCD, and/or Depression* (Raskin, 2022), Raskin has a lot of street cred, in my opinion, and her proverbial jab landed (a bit masochistically, I admit) with me; I had to read on. I was most intrigued because she pinpoints a theme in lots of OCD treatments these days.

What bearing does your childhood, or the past itself, have on your OCD in the first place? Isn't it just a biobehavioral thing you want to manage and embrace, and then move on with your day?

Raskin proceeds to tell us that in a recent couples counseling session she lamented how obsessively anxious and fearful she had become about not being as successful in her career now, in her thirties, as she had been in her twenties. She bemoaned: "Why am I not getting as much engagement as I did in the past? Am I losing that special something?" Soon Raskin had gone full-tilt into a thought spiral: "What-if I've just transferred all the anxiety and fear around finding a life partner to worrying about my career?"

Raskin surprised herself by not punching out her own therapist when he asked her a question she would normally despise: "*Why* have you always been so fixated on being successful in your career?" Raskin didn't expect to have any answer, but something welled up. She reflected on how, growing up with OCD from the age of four, she felt:

> crazy, out of control, and unlikable. But the one thing I did have in my corner was that I excelled at school and extracurricular activities. I might not have been able to get a boyfriend or maintain a healthy friendship, but I did win an American History award and got to play junior varsity tennis when I was still in middle school. As much as I mentally and emotionally struggled, there was always external validation that I was "important." (para. 4)

And it dawned on her that her obsessions were protecting her from some big emotions that might just be a knockout punch. They were continually sparring inside her skull: "I might be insane, but at least, I'm special."

There was more nuance there! There was a hidden wisdom in the obsessions themselves, and yet neurotically, while they pointed to one thing—you need to be successful—they were also avoiding the more visceral and profound struggle: it's hard to feel small and like a loser and still find a way to save face. External validation and praise became her obsessive-compulsive way to avoid the feelings that, ironically, might set her free, if only they could be confronted.

And yet, if she only looked at her OCD as random, intrusive thoughts, she might have never put this together. If she hadn't looked at how the past was repeating itself in her present and, in its own unexpected way, was trying to help her as much as it persecuted her, she might not have found this clarity. While she started off as the prizefighter knocking me out with her first words, she was now on the floor, voluntarily. She was surrendering to the deeper reservoirs of feeling that OCD makes us privy too and finding a way to give them a voice.

As we've seen in both multiplicity and IFS terms, obsessions and compulsions are the protectors, managers, and firefighters trying to dissociate those "bad-me" sides of self because they are quite difficult to integrate without boatloads of compassion and curiosity. They are actually wonderful sides of self that need to be restored in their proper places, and to be understood in context in order to feel (and be) truly strong. And as I hope you can also see, there's something much more impactful than merely taking a literal stance on obsessions: without a rhyme and reason, with a metaphorical understanding of what they symbolize, you have much less power to fight your OCD. And worse than losing that fight, you'll never have the joy of learning to embrace what has seemed to be your opponent and end the needless fight once and for all.

PRESUME GUILT, PROVE YOUR INNOCENCE

I once heard OCD advocate Reverend Katie O'Dunne (2023a) share an important truth about OCD that she received from writer Shala Nicely (2018). OCD operates under the assumption that you are presumed guilty until proven innocent. OCD will make you search for an alibi while constantly taunting you with your guilt. O'Dunne dramatizes how OCD positions you as prosecutor and defense attorney, as judge and jury. Her advice, consistent with conventional ERP and ACT, is to leave the courtroom. Engaging the drama of this dilemma *is* the dilemma itself, nothing less and nothing more.

My view is a bit different and moves us out of the courtroom into the imagination. Learning how to incorporate the important messages within OCD is crucial. It is like an old Talmudic expression, "An uninterpreted dream is like an unopened letter from God."

When we get to the nuance, we can interpret the dream in a meaningful way and not get caught up in the exaggerated stuff that seems like nonsense. That's a both/and approach to both claiming all the good inside and being bad and brash, too.

Singer-songwriter-poet Leonard Cohen once wrote: "If you don't become the ocean, you'll be seasick every day" (2000). His metaphor is a lifesaver when you're caught in the undertow of OCD. One of the hidden rules of OCD is that you should be in control of every thought and feeling (Rockwell-Evans, 2023) and that you must be good, too. When you are compelled by this rule, you get caught up in all of the *negativity*, and you completely forget about the possible *nuance*.

Happily, life is much more complex, dynamic, and interesting than OCD can make it seem. And like Leonard Cohen, who himself learned how to use mindfulness and meditation to overcome his lifelong depression, we begin to embrace the internal ocean.

In that internal ocean, your feelings and thoughts, whether they are bad, good, or something in between, have their right and reason to be wherever they need to be. Instead of trying to control them and becoming seasick every day, you can learn how to embrace the ocean and become like it. You can learn how to float calmly on it when it's gentle, you can learn how to surf when it's wavy, and you can learn how to swim parallel to the shore when the riptide tries to pull you in and under.

EXERCISES

From Negative to Nuance: Turning Thought Spirals into Virtuous Circles

With OCD, there's a tendency to rush into what-if thought spirals and then quickly counteract them with the if-then magic of compulsions. In this chapter, you've seen several examples of how helpful it is to transform the negative into nuance, and how doing so reconnects you to the imaginative possibility of a new kind of what-if: the *virtuous circle*.

You've seen Greta Thunberg, John Green, Joe Alterman, Cristi López, and Allison Raskin make this shift and lean into the nuance that is waiting to be reclaimed by engaging their OCD in new ways. In this exercise, you're going to identify your default ways of going to the negative and remind yourself of new ways to, instead, court nuance.

How do you do this? The first step is to be curious and alert to all of the feelings you are experiencing, even if they seem to conflict with and contradict each other.

Alexandra felt both excited and confident about her research findings but then was quickly disappointed, angry, and scared about her mentor's negative response. Because these didn't seem to jive easily, she started to focus only on the negative—her research ideas were wrong, she couldn't trust her own perceptions, and she would lose the approval of and connection with her highly admired mentor.

Is your current thought spiral—whether it's around doubting yourself, being afraid of catching or spreading a disease, fearing contamination, whether this is the perfect relationship for you, whether you are truly a bad person—are there any hidden mixtures of nuanced feelings that you're not giving space for?

Are you feeling tired, angry, hungry, disappointed, ambivalent, or any other mixture of feelings that are difficult to be with in a nuanced way? Are you having taboo feelings about an important person in your life such as your significant other, family member, teacher, boss, or best friend?

If either of these are true, freewrite some of the mixture of feelings you are having about yourself, a person, or a particular triggering situation, and see if it leads you toward a virtuous circle instead of down a thought spiral.

Like jazz pianist Joe Alterman or painter Cristi López, is there a creative venture (or ventures) where you can direct some of the nuance and complexity that is begging to find form in you?

If you can be with and notice more nuance with an enhanced curiosity and interest, try to see if you can incorporate it into your work like Cristi López has. Remember how she used the scissors, which symbolize her fear of accidentally hurting her family, as a tool for recognizing her own healthy, perceptive sharpness and even her power to not be overtaken by fear.

Joe found that jazz gave him more permission to follow the fullness of his feeling and thought, and to find mentors who could support him in putting it into play. Are there any mentors in the form of teachers, coaches, family, or friends who help you put this nuance into interesting form?

How to Be an Asshole (And Not *Really Be an Asshole!*)

It takes getting more comfortable with exercising your bad, brash self to move from the negative into the nuance. In this exercise, I playfully invite you to be a little bit of a rebel, or even an asshole, and entertain what it's like to move outside of the inner pressure you feel to be "good" at every turn.

So you didn't anticipate everything and make sure that you didn't sleepwalk with scissors, you didn't make sure that when your call accidentally dropped that you didn't totally offend the friend you were talking to, or some other variation of making sure everything was okay even though it was never really in your control to begin with. You're human, and sometimes you're not perfectly good. Sometimes it's because of circumstances, and sometimes it's because you also have your own needs you're trying to balance out.

When I told my client Tristan to be more of an asshole next week, he came back to the next session and said, "Mike, you didn't *really* mean for me to be an asshole, did you? I'm just not so okay with that but maybe I misunderstood you."

Conjuring Augustus from *The Fault in Our Stars*, I said, "Nah, I didn't really mean for you to really be an asshole, it was a metaphor.

I just want you to befriend your rebellious trickster side and engage him with more curiosity and passion."

"But what's the benefit of being a pseudo-asshole? I mean, how does that really help me?"

"It's going to give you more experience with being with those 'bad' sides more comfortably, so your OCD doesn't co-opt them. And then you can have a lot more fun and control over it than what OCD does to you."

What thoughts, feelings, and behaviors that you associate with being a "total asshole" can you stand to try out a little more in a playful and slightly subversive manner?

What about these "bad" sides make you feel nervous, uncomfortable, or fearful? Maybe it makes you feel like a totally selfish or rotten person. You might feel like you're not tuning in enough to how others feel or are impacted by you. It might scare you to feel so much power and confidence—who am I to lord over anyone and take up so much space? But remember, it's vital for you to be a little bad and brash. Owning your healthy wild side is part of the "selfish empathy" you need to take fuller ownership of yourself. And rest assured, all of those strong "good" sides will temper these sides beautifully and give you the fullness and range you deserve to enjoy.

4

OCD DOES YOUR DIRTY WORK

Although he was never diagnosed with OCD, this notable man in psychological history certainly was meticulous and obsessional in manner and thinking. He ate lunch daily at the stroke of 1 p.m. (so precisely you could set your clock by him!), composed more than ten thousand letters to friends and colleagues, and obsessively explored new landscapes of human functioning from the nature of consciousness and dreams to the origins of psychological distress. A patient of his, and one of the early twentieth-century's famous OCD cases, a twenty-nine-year-old named Paul L.—later known, dramatically, as "the Ratman"—confessed that he felt at home in his hands as a physician because his explanations reminded him so much of his own obsessional streams of consciousness.

We are talking of none other than Sigmund Freud, a man's whose ideas on OCD have been largely discredited even though they have much to offer in our quest to understand and heal it (Freud, 1963). The baby has been thrown out with the bathwater regarding Freud's work on OCD, and we have much to gain by correcting this in the pages ahead.

Using his ideas, I'll show how OCD does important "dirty work" for you, stepping in to establish clearer and healthier boundaries in your personal and work relationships. Unfortunately, with your highly developed empathy, you feel overly responsible for others at the expense of yourself. Boundaries become blurry.

OCD starts as a helper but becomes a devil's bargain, serving as a spokesperson for the internal conflicts that most OCD specialists never talk about. I'll show how to identify the metaphorical messages within your OCD, and how to cultivate "selfish empathy"—the capacity to hold equal space for yourself and others.

All the seeming negativity we visited in the previous chapter will get converted into nuance, but with a focus on healthier, more satisfying relationships. We'll see how unfamiliar yet refreshing it is to be "brash and bad" and how important this is for a more flexible, differentiated, and confident you.

I'll illustrate the main tools for finding the upside through the story of Angela's surprising obsession with having and then healing her "brain damage" and through the story of Elizabeth the opera singer literally losing and finding her voice again. We'll also revisit Freud's famous case of Paul L. to learn how you can empower yourself to take on OCD's dirty work, and not need its "help" any longer.

THE HEALTHY BACK-AND-FORTH OF BOUNDARIES

Poet Robert Frost once quipped: "Look! First, I want to be a person. And I want you to be a person, and then we can be as interpersonal as you please. We can pull each other's noses—do all sorts of things" (1931). Rabbi Hillel echoes the centrality of balancing self-care with service to others with his phrase: "If I am not for myself, who will be for me? If I am only for myself, what am I? And if not now, when?" (Zlotowitz & Scherman, 1999, p. 1).

Healthy boundaries require this "selfish empathy," the capacity to say yes and no to others in nuanced and sophisticated ways (Tawwab, 2021). These boundaries are porous enough to be moved by others and the world, but semipermeable enough—just like all of the cells in our bodies—to assure that your interests are well protected.

With OCD, tending to your inner feelings while maintaining your outside relationships (as a highly empathetic person) pulls at you constantly. "Pulling at the other's nose" seems troubling and scary. Dangerous. Almost unthinkable.

In chapters 2 and 3, I focused on the parts of OCD that are hardwired into your *nature* and temperament—a highly sensitive and generous heart combined with a wildly imaginative and expansive mind. In this chapter, I'll focus on *nurture*—how and why OCD plays itself out in early and current relationships. Learning to balance magically close connections with others while standing firm as a separate and differentiated individual is an essential task when you have OCD.

IF YOU DON'T STOP, I'LL GET BRAIN DAMAGE: PEOPLE-PLEASING PROTECTION

Boundary Strategy 1. My Mind Must Protect and Punish Me

Angela loved working at a nonprofit whose mission was aligned with her Catholic faith. She liked being behind the scenes coordinating food drives and speaking with community partners to share lists of helpful resources for the homeless and the mentally ill, and, above all, she reveled in giving. Whether coordinating food deliveries to the elderly in winter or to families who couldn't pay their rent, she delighted in filling a role that fit so perfectly with the values she learned in church growing up.

Yet, she couldn't reconcile her faith with what she learned about the Catholic Church from the news. Sexual abuse scandals were cropping up left and right in the early 2000s and it was terribly disillusioning and upsetting. However, Angela believed there must still be goodness there. The kindly and patient nuns and priests had been a refuge from the abuse Angela experienced at the hands of her mother. For her, the Church *had* to be good, and she *must* overcompensate for any of its badness.

You could say Angela had the reverse tack of rock star Sinead O'Connor (Hess, 2021) who called out the church in the early 1990s. O'Connor was no stranger to abuse either. Her mother, a devout Catholic, had been her perpetrator for years, and on her eighteenth birthday when her mother passed, she took down and obliterated the one photograph her mother elevated in her room (Hess, 2021).

It was a foreshadowing of the prescient yet fateful moment on *Saturday Night Live* when O'Connor became a pariah for tearing apart the pope's image in front of a stunned live audience. O'Connor was a rebel quickly punished for living her truth, a truth that would soon be vindicated both by *Boston Globe* stories that shined a spotlight on the church sex abuse scandals and as a harbinger of the #MeToo movement later to follow.

The Sinead O'Connor route to addressing boundaries showcases the OCD sufferer's worst nightmare about rocking the boat, and how real and understandable the fear of being excommunicated is. Soon after her *SNL* moment, O'Connor was booed off stage and virtually "canceled." It was a bold, brash rebel move on her part. Ironically, OCD becomes an internal form of self-abuse and self-excommunication, punishing oneself as a form of atonement.

Despite her librarian's reserve, Angela had a playful side. She loved to joke around with her colleagues, and you could almost always hear her laugh trailing off at the end of each and every conversation. She had a good friend, Dennis, whom she worked closely with on many projects and, a quintessential New Yorker, he often riffed back and forth and gestured wildly in pantomime.

One day, he was jokingly teasing her. He innocuously tickled her on her forearms, and while she was laughing on the outside, a sinister obsession began to take hold inside: "If you don't stop now, I'll get brain damage."

Angela knew Dennis well and could easily recognize there was nothing truly hurtful, mean spirited, or even sexually untoward about the interchange. But at the same time, his behavior blurred a boundary.

Angela was so accustomed to giving. Not being selfless and generous even in a simple moment like this created inner conflict: she couldn't express that she didn't like the tickling and wanted it to stop. Instead, her OCD stepped in to create a boundary: her mind punished and protected her.

The exchange was over in a microsecond, and they resumed working together as usual. But inside, Angela obsessed over the possibility that she had been neurologically injured, and even though she knew it couldn't be the case, she wondered: did it cause brain damage?

Angela shared this in our session a few days after it occurred and was beside herself with worry and doubt. She had Googled to see if any isolated instances of tickling had ever led to brain damage and finding very rare instances made her panic.

In addition to going down the rabbit hole about her physical health, her fears morphed into an even more profound worry: was Dennis a sexual predator and she hadn't realized it until now? Was this a #MeToo moment for her? Was she foolish to trust her own instincts about his goodness and was she now responsible for potentially subjecting others to him? Was she failing the world just like her beloved Church had?

Angela's OCD was trying to do some important dirty work for her. First, it was alerting her, in an exaggerated and over-the-top way, that she needed space. What more destructive injury can one imagine than brain damage, after all? Her psyche was shouting at her: "You need and deserve boundaries!"

Second, because Angela needed to be "good at all turns"— remember, she had to compensate for the abuse she witnessed at home and in her beloved mother Church—she couldn't be too aggressive. So, her OCD stepped in and gave her a blameless maneuver. "You have to do this because you're under *my control.*" Angela wasn't asking Dennis to stop but, rather, her *OCD* was.

Can you see how OCD tries to "help" in this strange way? It does something quite poetic, if you can recall Frost's definition: "poetry is the one permissible way of saying one thing and meaning another" (Frost, 1939). Of course, when you're experiencing it, it's not poetic at all. It's sinister, overbearing, and diabolical. But as you'll see, when we can work it this way, we can do so much more with it; your OCD becomes a valued messenger.

This is the side of the OCD equation that Freud was working so diligently on: its hidden conflicts and ambivalences. Who is friend and who is foe? Can I be good in this world even if I need to set boundaries with somebody I love? How do I reconcile that a person who should be loving can also be momentarily thoughtless or cruel?

We talk about OCD being ego-dystonic—that is, at odds with our values and what we really believe. OCD makes us worry about something that, on some rational level, we understand can't be true, but we just can't stop. But OCD also arrives for a purpose closer to your heart: to justify the need for healthy boundaries. Like we saw in the previous chapter, OCD sufferers shy away from being brash out of fear or guilt. This aspect of self must be reintegrated with support.

OCD does the "dirty work" of asserting the self. It makes sure not to hurt the other person, of course, and simultaneously, it provides you with the control you crave. "You have to stop because if you don't, my OCD tells me I'll get brain damage." It's not me that is demanding it, it is my OCD.

The fire needed to express and protect the self gets stolen by OCD. Not feeling entitled to their own space and opinions, those with OCD quickly doubt themselves and seek reassurance. Those they care about must be okay in order for them to be okay. Unable to stand alone, they lose the joy of being "as interpersonal as they please."

GOOD TROUBLE

You might be familiar with civil rights icon and US representative John Lewis. On March 7, 1965, twenty-five-year-old Lewis "gave a little blood" on the Edmund Pettus Bridge in Selma, Alabama, for the right to vote (Porter, 2020). Throughout his life of service and activism, he talked about how this fit within his concept of causing *good trouble*.

"Good trouble" is doing what is necessary, important, and even noble in the face of what is unjust. At face value, it might sound problematic or even wrong—trouble isn't something most people aspire to, after all. But this trouble is tempered with goodness, nuance, and humanity. A wonderful paradox, good trouble operates from a place of love for something bigger while speaking out against what keeps you down and prevents you from actualizing your fullest self.

As a young man when he walked on Edmund Petkus Bridge, John Lewis spoke about the need to keep loving the people who deny you service. OCD too tries to deny you your equal rights to be fully integrated and connected, and your role is to push back with some "good trouble" to get yourself back.

This is the theme of this chapter—how to establish better boundaries, why it's so hard to do, and, yet, why it's so necessary to cause good trouble with your psyche. It's about more than just desensitizing yourself to your OCD symptom *du jour*. It's about using your sensitivity in service of healthy assertiveness. It's about reclaiming your full voice.

FINDING HER VOICE AGAIN

Boundary Strategy 2. I Will Cut Off Connection to My Body/Feelings

Elizabeth came into my office with the winsome smile and bright blue eyes that sparkled onstage, and then, remembering the comfort of the space, she allowed the worry on her brow to settle in. She had lost it again. It was the third time this week that she went to practice singing a passage from an aria and nothing came forth. The strength, vibrancy, and passion that she could harness in her soprano voice was missing and nowhere to be found.

She had been listening to her teacher's instructions, watching her vowels, gathering air from her diaphragm, and seeing the musical line float before her eyes as she began to execute each phrase. But it wasn't working.

Riddled with tension in her throat, her anxiety kept gathering to the point of a panic attack, and Elizabeth was so embarrassed that she had run from the practice room. "What is happening to me?" she implored. "Can you give me any relaxation or breathing techniques or some kind of first aid for these panic attacks? I just don't know what to do!"

Elizabeth couldn't stop her OCD from flaring up. She obsessed about which strategy would be just right for getting her voice back, perpetually asked for reassurance that she had chosen the right career and began to tailspin about how quitting singing might devastate her family and waste their money on a degree that she might never be able to use.

In keeping with our conversation here about boundaries, Elizabeth sensitively took on the feelings of her teacher and couldn't sort through which were truly her own. She was preoccupied with pleasing her teacher, and, even more, she sensed her teacher's narcissistic need to be successful.

Her teacher couldn't stomach feeling like a failure, unconsciously bristling at the raw and honest vulnerability that Elizabeth exhibited, defensively scolding her, "Stop giving yourself away so much." Elizabeth didn't have a problem with vulnerability, but the blurriness of the situation made that hard to see. Instead, she attacked herself.

Elizabeth was no stranger to taking care of others' insecurities and anxieties. She became a pro from an early age, noticing her mother's fears of being alone. Her mother's father died at an early age and, subsequently she was ever vigilant about the slightest rupture in a relationship that might portend the inevitable. And as a result, Elizabeth's mother developed an elaborate set of obsessive-compulsive rituals to make sure that all of her children were within eyesight, physically keeping bathroom doors ajar lest someone slip away and constantly obsessing about the family members' safety if they so much as went to the local store.

Elizabeth was proficient at taking care of her mother's traumatically informed neuroses and was an easy magnet for her teacher's narcissistic fears as well. Instead of focusing on her own voice, she felt the tension and unexpressed fear and terror of those who were supposed to be mentoring and nurturing her. And this rightfully terrified her now too. Singing had become a matter of life or death.

To healthily align her back with her own authority, I said, "I think you are losing connection with your own voice and story and are getting easily recruited into taking care of your teacher's, just like you had to with your mother. But wait a second—you have the right to have your voice here!"

Encouraging her with both tenderness and fire, I continued, "And it makes total sense why you would be so caring and sensitive to your teacher's needs. Your capacity to really listen and be sensitive to tone is what makes you such a wonderful singer. And yet, we need to also make sure you don't take ownership for what is their tension and not yours!"

She perked up and a little glimmer of chutzpah came out. "Yeah, you're right! I never thought of it like that. I always thought I just had to go along with my teachers and family because I needed them so much. What if you're right? What if they needed me more than I thought?"

"That's right. What if you had more strength than you actually knew? What if that's your secret superpower? That's what you deserve to tap into to get your voice back again. And it's yours for the taking!" I smiled as if with a verbal wink that said, "Isn't this great news?"

All of a sudden, I could hear the force and strength come back into her voice, and she began to perk up like a flower that had just found the sun.

Elizabeth literally and metaphorically lost her voice (and her authority) because her compulsion to accommodate her teacher's issues, just as she did with her mother in her family of origin, superseded accommodating her own needs. Our work together enabled her to remain sensitively tuned into her teacher without losing herself or her own voice. It sharpened and clarified her own agency as distinct from others' in a way that empowered her. She mastered "selfish empathy."

OCD forms when it feels impossible to integrate parallel truths. While the OCD ends up tormenting you and gaining a monstrous life of its own, initially, it is simply attempting to take on whatever intensity needs to be recognized but cannot yet be assimilated.

This is the wisdom of OCD. In addition to persecuting you, it is attempting to show you what clearer boundaries might look like. Now, you have no choice but to see where good and bad exist; blurriness becomes unthinkable. Unfortunately, because OCD is unconscious and reactive, it doesn't regulate boundaries in a nuanced way, but you can.

It truly is a gift to be as sensitive and strongly tuned into others. It takes an embodied connection and healing, often through a therapeutic relationship, to integrate it. This is the power of transforming the negativity into nuance and the miraculous, vast imagination we've been talking about—this is the upside.

GETTING BEYOND SOPHIE'S CHOICE

Boundary Strategy 3. I Will Overcompensate and Explode

I recently had a supervisee named Jeff. He was not only a superbly tuned-in therapist but had also struggled with OCD all his life. He was especially sensitive to those with OCD, but his recent client, Alyssa, a forty-two-year-old lawyer was a bit different. In addition to OCD, she had a history of severe physical and emotional trauma. She described her childhood home as having an uncanny similarity to that in Roald Dahl's book *Matilda* (Dahl, 2013).

In Dahl's story, Matilda is a precocious and perspicacious little girl who is already reading *Great Expectations* and *Jane Eyre* by age four and can see through the emotional immaturity and insecurity of her sadistic and envious parents, Mr. and Mrs. Wormwood. Matilda's parents refuse to acknowledge her true capacities and instead mock her, while she attempts to keep herself sane by pulling pranks on them like gluing her father's hat to his head, placing a parrot in the chimney to simulate a ghost, and bleaching her father's hair blonde with peroxide. Later in the story, she develops the supernatural power of telekinesis, which she uses to confront the similarly abusive headmistress with carefully worded messages from her dead father.

Alyssa's parents were much like the Wormwoods, detesting and disdaining Alyssa's easy capacity to read energies, her deep sensitivity to both the human and animal world, and her growing capacity for clairvoyant dreams. In one heartbreaking incident, they knowingly shot at a regularly visiting cardinal and bluebird to whom Alyssa had grown quite attached. These mere "things with feathers" represented, as Emily Dickinson (2016) might agree, all of the hope that Alyssa could grasp in her oppressive home.

When the birds were killed, something inside of Alyssa went into hiding and, from that point forward, she regularly dissociated and cut off from the world in catatonic fits. These dissociative moments were intensified by the regular beating she received as more retaliation for the sensitivity that her parents couldn't tolerate. Both parents, themselves, had been physically and emotionally abused as children but they never had something that held hope for them like the birds did for Alyssa.

In some meetings, Jeff felt like Alyssa was silent and waiting for him to squirm while he felt her frustration and anger about how he was messing it all up. He could feel the seething rage that she likely never ever had the luxury and safety to proclaim in her family of origin—she would be beaten even more severely if she had—but he started to feel angry himself.

One day, a staring contest, which is what their Zoom sessions seemed to be comprised of—who would blink first?—erupted when Jeff couldn't take it anymore.

"Would you cut the shit and just tell me already how angry you are with me? You don't have to torture me like this." Jeff didn't know where this came from and, pretty soon afterward, he felt tremendously guilty.

Wasn't he supposed to be the therapist modeling how to have emotional regulation and unconditional positive regard? Wasn't he supposed to be the professional here and not lose his cool? Jeff started to castigate himself internally, and he noticed that old OCD symptoms of guilt and shame were cropping up.

It was the way he felt when his mother was emotionally insensitive with him as a child. He couldn't stand living on edge, afraid of what might set her off, while forever waiting his turn to be nurtured.

Up until this point in their therapy, Jeff took on the role that Miss Honey did for Matilda. As her name suggests, Miss Honey is the warm and kind teacher who befriends and advocates for Matilda against her abusive parents, trying to help them see her great gifts. She is also the foil to the sadistic headmistress who delights in over-the-top punishments for the children.

In supervision, I could tell Jeff felt like he had made an error and crossed a line. His boundaries weren't good, he told me. His emotions got the best of him. He didn't know how to be as receptive and loving while feeling so annoyed and unhappy; how could he safely say what was affecting him too?

This is the *Sophie's Choice* (Styron, 1992) dilemma that many people with OCD feel—do I choose myself and kill the person I love the most, or do I disappoint and kill the person I love and need and neglect myself? It's a terrible position to be in, but there is a way out.

I surprised Jeff with my response: "Yeah, but she seemed to deserve it. You were just calling the hard foul and the penalty on her. It's okay for her to be hurt and angry at you, but there's a limit. It's sadistic to keep taking it out on you."

Jeff's self-criticism made him lose touch with the fuller picture. He had been extremely sensitive and kind and understanding of the trauma Alyssa suffered, both in her family of origin and in relationships (including with him), but he was rightfully picking up on something destructive that she was doing as well: obliterating him as she had been by her parents as a child.

I reminded Jeff that he could tune in deeply to her *and* himself by bringing these points together in a more nuanced way, "Alyssa, I can feel how deeply enraged you are when I disappoint you and how it hurts you so much that it seems like your only option is to shut me out, just like you have dissociated in the past. But I can't just be your punching bag at those moments because I have a self that gets affected by it. I can certainly talk these issues out, but to be brought back in as a stand-in to punish is neither empowering for you nor fair to me. There is another way."

It was a bold move, but it would help Alyssa move into the grief and pain underlying her trauma and help her humanize it. It would save her from becoming a *divine victim*.

Jeff could still find connection with her suffering and be healthily entitled to his own right to self-preservation. He could showcase how to use healthy aggression and healthy hate joined with ferocious love and tenderness. It would be both/and instead of either/or, respecting the complexity and nuance of each of them, and witnessing both her trauma and the way back to hope.

GETTING BEYOND A DEVIL'S BARGAIN: TAMING THE FOX

Boundary Strategy 4. I Will Avoid and Be Perfectly Self-Sufficient

This next boundary strategy is a devil's bargain. It will give you perfection (or really the illusion of perfection), but it will take your soul. Like Peter Pan (Barrie, 2022), it convinces you that it's possible to have no boundaries and no shadow. You are limitless and can metaphorically fly in whatever situation you need.

However, you'll quickly come up against the rub that without reality, fulfilling and creative living isn't possible. Although magical, it's just a facsimile. This obsessional, all-or-nothing approach to life is unsustainable in a world where boundaries are essential.

Happily, there's a way to transform it so that you can get yourself back through relationships, which provides the healthiest limits and boundaries. They will domesticate and tame you as they did for twenty-eight-year-old David with his manager at work.

David had started a new job at a think-tank in Washington, DC. He was excited because it married everything he loved: politics, philosophy, and writing. But like in graduate school, when he had to write in-depth research papers, his "comprehensiveness" OCD reawakened. He needed to have everything in his writing and thinking, and if he didn't, he always had the perfect backup strategy: avoidance.

I myself know the strange and perverse beauty of this particular variation of OCD. When I was in high school and college, I took copious notes and always felt pangs of guilt if I hadn't transcribed the essence of what the teachers—and even sometimes what classmates—said. It felt magical in its own way, being graced with receiving word from on high from teachers whom I so respected. But if I didn't record it correctly or missed out on some golden nugget, all felt gone, like the great knowledge of civilizations past had somehow been lost to the ages. It was a tremendous weight to carry, but as you'd imagine, it also had a lot of functional benefits, leading me to be a high-achieving and successful student.

I was so driven there wasn't space to miss anything. True to the rules of OCD, as writer/therapist Kim Rockwell-Evans (2023) has beautifully distilled, I needed to be in 100 percent control on the outside. Inside, I felt helpless and adrift. It masked the terror at the root of it all: loss. If I never lost knowledge, God could still be in his heaven, and everything would be well with the world.

My case was almost opposite to David. David had a habit of not asking too many questions to his supervisors and colleagues, and instead felt that he should be able to decipher all that needed to be accomplished on a given task. At times, even though he was quoting others' work in his department, he felt compelled to do his own research to assure that their statements and findings all checked out and were annotated correctly.

David might have gotten away without being discovered, much as my own OCD fell under the radar in school, had it not been for his boss, Sam. Sam took a liking to David's methodical and richly drawn writing that blended political philosophy with current events in a unique way. He also saw a bit of himself in the twenty-something and one day ventured: "Hey David, let me ask you something. You're an amazing writer, have you ever struggled with being *too good* a writer? When I was starting out, I was a bit of a perfectionist myself and my OCD kinda took over. I'd try all sorts of ways of getting past my supervisors even though I was terrified that one day they'd find me out."

David was stunned, but now there was no way for him to keep all of these abstract demands and wishes only in his head. It had always felt like the game inside him was programmed to make sure he was self-sufficient at all costs. He told himself, "Don't let them see that you don't know something, research as much as you can if you're starting to be unsure, and in the worst-case scenario, just avoid doing the work."

David had been a victim of this last strategy way too many times in his college career. Even though he might have been able to speak backward and forward about a particular philosopher, when it came to writing, he would have epic writer's block and couldn't even produce a word. He had taken so many withdrawals and medical leaves from classes that he couldn't keep track. The game had always been to be perfectly self-sufficient or avoid doing anything at all. Avoidance held on to potential perfection, at the very least.

But when Sam gently invited him to speak about himself, he found a face-saving way to begin a dialogue with him. It helped that Sam knew how OCD worked, that it was a unique kind of frenemy—one you always want to hate but you also have to love in some way.

And Sam himself let David off the hook, technically speaking, by reminding him that he didn't need to be responsible for the research in his department but, instead, he was actually helping to make it more accessible and presentable for a public audience.

Sam told him about a story that helped him get through his own fears of being so self-sufficient and perfectionistic as well. It was the warm and inviting story of the Fox from de Saint-Exupery's book *The Little Prince* (1971).

In the story, the Fox pleads with the prince to tame him so that he can feel safe enough to play. The Little Prince doesn't, at first, understand what taming is and why it's even necessary. The Fox tells him that it is to establish ties and connection and that it is this need that makes us special to each other. Taming, he says, is the only way one truly understands things (de Saint-Exupery, 1971).

He shows him that, each day, "First you will sit down at a little distance from me—like that—in the grass. I shall look at you out of the corner of my eye, and you will say nothing. Words are the source of misunderstandings. But you will sit a little closer to me, every day" (p. 47).

Not only will the Fox grow to feel safe and closer with the Little Prince but a new ritual will emerge that is much more interesting and flexible. The Fox will come to get excited about the Little Prince's habitual return at 4:00 p.m. each day and will also begin to imagine seeing his blonde hair in the swaying of the wheat field.

This crescendo to the Fox's great secret, which is also the antidote for the OCD tendencies that overplay in the mind. "And now here is my secret, a very simple secret: It is only with the heart that one can see rightly; what is essential is invisible to the eye" (p. 48).

In other words, Sam is telling David that it is this need to work and play together that will allow them each to know each other a little more. And in so doing, each won't have to be so perfect and impersonal but can instead be real and safe together.

David understood how different this more embodied and related safety could be than the abstract safety he felt in his head by compelling himself on and on, way past his bedtime, to make sure he had researched every last piece of evidence for a particular report.

David learned and felt, in his new, more vulnerable and connected relationship with his supervisor, Sam, that one can feel even more at peace and in connection through the heart and soul. It didn't have to come in the abstract perfection of his self-sufficiency but in the interdependent dance of being tamed.

As a devil's bargain, OCD will give you perfection, but it will take your soul. A soul*ful* connection comes through relationships that tame us.

REVISITING THE RATMAN

Boundary Strategy 5. The Combination Special

In a 1988 interview, singer-songwriter Leonard Cohen revealed the heart of his famous song: "This world is full of conflicts and full of things that cannot be reconciled, but there are moments when we can transcend the dualistic system and reconcile and embrace the whole mess, and that's what I mean by 'Hallelujah.'" As we'll see in a reworking of a case, below, the heart of OCD treatment is cultivating these hallelujah moments too.

Freud's work with Paul L., the Ratman, helps him arrive at the central features of psychodynamic theory: the lasting impact of early childhood experiences, the inevitability of emotional conflict, the psyche's resourceful ways of expressing and disguising pain, and how taboo sexual and aggressive impulses challenge one's morals and social connections.

But most people don't realize that Freud helps us better understand the emotional and relational context that gets you to the upside of OCD. He illustrates the highly porous boundary between the OCD sufferer and attachment figures (parents in early life and romantic partners in adulthood) and keys into the significant ambivalence that is so hard for OCD sufferers to resolve without proper support.

Like a character in a good novel, in Paul's case, we have all the elements of a complex human dilemma: How can I carry my own power and self-interest, and also be responsibly deferential to those I love and admire? How can I hold on to my identity even when it conflicts with my family or culture? Is it possible to use hate or desire constructively or must I protect myself from them? Power, identity, love, and hate are all seen through the prism of negative uncertainties instead of the lens of nuanced possibilities we've been tracking together.

Nowhere are these questions more apparent than at the beginning of Paul L.'s case. The "morbid idea" (Freud, 1963) that his parents know his thoughts—particularly his early developing sexual curiosity—is the inciting incident for his OCD. Paul's guild-laden fear of his inner thoughts being seen in some omnipotent way by others is a common feature of the blurred boundaries that haunt so many with OCD: Will I be found out? Will someone catch all the taboo thoughts that go through my head? Will I be able to control these powers, or will they bring my downfall?

Freud notes the intense closeness Paul has with caretakers and romantic objects and his simultaneous concerns about inevitable hostilities and resentments. Paul L. loves his father "more than anybody in the world" and will sacrifice his own happiness to keep him alive, describing their closeness as a "greater intimacy than between best friends" (Freud, 1963, p. 26) Simultaneously, his unconscious hostility toward him is represented in the sadistic obsession of a rat burrowing up his father's anus in accordance with a practice of torture used for prisoners of war that he learned about in his travels as a soldier.

Paul is preoccupied with thoughts about his father's death. He secretly imagines that if his father dies, he will gain the sympathy of the woman he loves and will become rich from his inheritance. He obsesses that "If I have this wish to see a woman naked, my father will have to die" or "If I do not pay back Lieutenant A., then the rat torture will come true for both my father and my lady" (Freud, 1963, p. 10).

The most stunning thing about Paul's full-blown case of OCD is how many of our different boundary strategies he uses. He uses his mind to protect and punish himself in a series of tortuous obsessions and compulsions like Angela (if he doesn't give money to the proper person, pray in a certain way, or think along the right lines, his father or his love interest will die), cuts himself off from his bodily desires and feelings like Elizabeth (suppressing his sexual and emotional desire, his aggression, and his decisive authority), overcompensates and explodes like Jeff (taking a razor to his throat when he is disgusted by the eruption of his taboo feelings), and attempts to be wholly self-sufficient like David (everything must be neatly figured out in his mind or else!).

The blurry boundaries that we see as an issue for so many, if not all, of those with OCD is front and center. True to form as a people-pleaser, Paul recounts his sexual history from childhood to adulthood in extraordinary detail—that is, his sexual explorations and curiosity as a child, his history of masturbation, and so forth. When asked why he chose to begin like this, he confesses to knowing Freud's theories. With that emotional sixth sense so characteristic of OCD, Paul instinctively fits his own experience into what is most "needed" from him.

Blurred boundaries also figure in Paul's low self-confidence. Paul's first recollection is of how much he needed reassurance from friends in his youth about his goodness and moral character, compulsively recruiting them to soothe the criminal impulses that tormented him.

As Paul's case moves forward, it's not surprising that he becomes preoccupied by both his desire and fear of sexuality and aggression. Sexuality and aggression are intimately connected to self-interest and are the most difficult to reconcile with the extraordinary empathic and moral sensibility of the OCD sufferer. As we'll see in the next chapter, in Mara Wilson's Junior Anti-Sex League, these highly charged, primal issues can't be managed through the mind alone.

Containing and expressing the two opposite and equal forces of love and hate are at the relational center of OCD. When he was around three or four, according to his mother's recollection, Paul bit his nurse, which brought on a beating from his father. Although he knew no bad language yet, Paul went into a "terrible rage while under the blows of his father," hurling insults in the form of common objects, screaming: "You lamp! You towel! You plate" (Freud, 1963, p. 46). His father, "so shaken by this outburst of elemental fury," stopped beating him and declared: "This child will either be a great man or a great criminal!" This scene had made such a memorable image on him that his father never beat him again. Paul himself became a coward out of fear of his own rage (Freud, 1963, p. 46).

Notice the either/or formulation that Paul's father makes and how it supports the prototypical OCD view—you will either be saintly or evil—rather than the both/and approach we are arriving at here. The fire within Paul asserting himself in disagreement, as in his erotic life, gets converted into the sadistic torture of the rat symbolism. Paul loses touch with the full range of his emotional power and his will to assert himself.

If we could, how might we help Paul today? First, just like with Angela, we'd identify how his OCD is protecting and punishing him by keeping away feelings that seem too raw, overpowering, and potentially dangerous to the close relationships he so cherishes. We would have him befriend those sides of himself and give them credit for taking care of him until the smoldering fire of them could be more fully integrated.

As for the sides that shut down his feelings, like Elizabeth shares in common, we'd recognize how understandable it is to convert his own power into cowardice as he did as a young boy. His constant need for reassurance and persistent indecisiveness are connected to fears of being too sharp and "too much" in his own authority. We would use our relationship to practice taking on a new voice that is both considered and decisive.

Like I did with Jeff, we would show how he is overcompensating and unfairly suppressing his feelings, not allowing room for understandable human imperfection. Ironically, this leads, like Jeff's outburst, to Paul taking a razor to his throat. Similarly, like with David, a taming relationship could move him from living in a lonely world of omnipotence and self-sufficiency to one with true power and connection.

WHY IS OCD SO HARD TO DECODE?

Freud has much to say about the difficulty of resolving OCD, and while his earliest understandings center on resolving the Oedipus complex—developing a superego with morality and conscience tempered by a healthy connection to self-interest and pleasure—revising the Ratman case helps us to easily decode OCD's tricks.

Like we saw in the introduction with Lucas, OCD performs unusual sleights of hand, and Freud grokked how this strange magic worked. The traumatic issues that activate OCD are not forgotten but lose emotional power. Emotions are disconnected from not just thought but also from the relationship context that makes any sense and meaning out them. The fuller story gets lost and all mixed up.

"What remains is ideational content that is 'colorless' and seemingly unimportant" (Freud, 1963, p. 38). Paul's obsession about the rat torturing his love interest and his father is a magical distraction from a higher stakes issue: an unexpressed bombshell of a conflict in his family of origin. Almost comically, Paul recounts it without having any awareness that it has *any significance* whatsoever.

Here is the heart of the matter. Paul is keenly aware of the conflict his own father felt in marrying into a wealthy family or a girl of more "humble birth," and when he is placed in that same situation, he's cornered. Should he marry the wealthy woman like his father or strike out on his own path? Virtually impossible to reconcile, from this point forward, Paul finds unconscious motivations to procrastinate and postpone the completion of his education, so he won't be forced to make a choice. Instead of staying with this most significant conflict, his OCD takes him to the harrowing hell of the rat torture, an expression and obscurer of his bind.

OCD symptoms get both distorted and removed from their original context and then generalize in a way that makes it harder and harder to catch. Freud notes that part of this is in the time lapse that occurs between the precipitating event and the emergence of obsessions themselves as well as in the variety of ways obsessions change and distort. Like a virus, OCD mutates and capitalizes on whatever can provide it a source for propagation, but when we get clearer and sharper about the emotional and relational "why" of your OCD, we find the source of the original "infection."

As the Ratman case and Freud's work shows us, learning how to decode OCD's hidden riddles in order to manage and negotiate healthier boundaries is one of the most powerful ways to get back to the upside of OCD.

EXERCISES: OCD DOES YOUR DIRTY WORK

Obsessions and compulsions often arise in an interpersonal context to help you negotiate and create healthy boundaries. Most OCD treatments do not focus on this possible function of OCD and thus, you might not have any experience with noticing it on the radar.

In the following exercise, you will begin to make some connections between how your OCD attempts to help you clarify the boundaries between yourself and important relational figures in your life. Notice which of these boundary strategies you use most.

Boundary Strategy 1. My Mind Must Protect and Punish Me

As we saw in Angela's case, sometimes your OCD swoops in to provide a hard boundary when you don't feel comfortable and confident enough to do it yourself. The protective part is an attempt to help you make a healthy boundary. The punishing part compels you to obsess about something in order to make that boundary possible.

In Angela's case, obsession came up in dramatic fashion: if you don't stop touching me now, I'll get brain damage. It also went very quickly into other thought spirals like fears of her coworker being an abuser.

With the obsession you're now experiencing, determine if it might be trying to communicate that you need some immediate space emotionally, physically, or both. Also, note in your own words if you are feeling conflicted, uncomfortable, or fearful of setting the boundary.

Boundary Strategy 2. I Will Cut Off Connection to My Body/Feelings

In contrast to the first boundary strategy, which is more centered in your mind, this one goes straight for the body. In Elizabeth's case, she started to have difficulty singing and started to feel visceral anxiety in her body (as well as some residual thought spirals, but these were secondary).

This boundary strategy will have you start to doubt your experience and lose touch with the mixture of feelings inside. Are you feeling angry, disappointed, afraid, and so on? Elizabeth couldn't be directly in touch with these feelings because she felt overly responsible for regulating the feelings of her teacher.

In this scenario, it helps to connect with your healthy voice and fire, like Elizabeth did, and to try to give form to it so you can get back to your visceral embodied experience. By doing this and by recognizing how much you feel responsible for taking care of another person, you will organically find ways of negotiating both.

Boundary Strategy 3: I Will Overcompensate and Explode

We saw this strategy with Jeff, who was trying to be as receptive and understanding as possible while feeling overrun and obliterated by his client's disowned aggression. In this scenario, you try to maintain a boundary by being as good as possible—by being a good listener, as Jeff did, or by being super tuned in to the needs of the other—but after too much intensity and time, you just can't do it.

The explosion of frustration and anger not only feels surprising and out of character but you might also feel guilty about losing it, as Jeff did. Show yourself compassion, as it's okay to have to notice and create room for your feelings, especially if they feel poorly attended to, minimized, or ignored.

In this scenario, it helps to notice how perfectionistic and unfair to the other person or even to yourself it is to hold in so much.

Boundary Strategy 4. I Will Avoid and Be Perfectly Self-Sufficient

We saw this strategy when David felt that he either had to know everything or avoid the situation all together. In this scenario, you are on the lookout for unnecessary pressure to be self-sufficient and fully in control and for phobic feelings about letting others know that you need support. Healthy taming, as we saw with the story of the Fox, makes a big difference here.

5

CARING FOR YOUR WILDNESS

It's not easy to care for the wildness within. If you have OCD, you know how vexing it is answer the insistent question poet Mary Oliver asks of us all: "Tell me, what is it you plan to do / With your one wild and precious life?" In this chapter, we're going to befriend your wild unconscious, but first things first, we must understand it in its natural habitat.

BEFRIENDING YOUR WILD UNCONSCIOUS

With his Queens, New York, accent and his borscht-belt delivery, psychologist and researcher Joel Weinberger always strikes me as the Jerry Seinfeld of the unconscious. You'd expect an expert like him to aggrandize the unconscious as the source of our deepest wisdom or to vilify it as the originator of our darkest impulses, but instead he teases you with: "There is no such thing as *the* unconscious, there's no little piece of your head separated from the rest of your head where your evil Mr. Hyde impulses live and there's no special part of your head where infinite wisdom really lives" (Weinberger, 2023).

Just as the quintessential *Seinfeld* television series (David & Seinfeld, 1989–1998) was a "show about nothing"—and yet in its satirical inventory of all the minutiae of social interactions, it was a show about everything—the unconscious, like Weinberger himself, is a trickster and a paradox. The unconscious is a "thing" both loved and reviled, known and unknown, and more than one hundred years on from Freud's first interest in it, researchers are finally putting scientific weight behind what is so difficult and important to understand about it. We've come a long way, baby!

Weinberger and his colleagues were among the few, if not the only, people to predict that Donald Trump would win the 2016 election, and they did so by tapping into and measuring the unconscious values of voters. The unconscious works fast and operates by associations, and it is often in contradiction to what our conscious minds say we think, feel, or believe. It's a design virtue that allows us to live with flexibility, complexity, and nuance.

So, is there really no such thing as the unconscious? Not exactly. Weinberger clarifies his larger point by proposing that it's more precise to say that the unconscious can't exist on its own. Defined by the interplay of what's conscious and what's not, what has been dubbed the unconscious is along the lines of the kind of both/and thinking we've been pursuing. As we'll see in this chapter, there's a lot we can learn about how to work with OCD by tracking this wild unconscious.

Recall that nuance so often distorts itself into negativity, especially, as we have seen, in the shape of obsessions and compulsions. In this chapter, we're going to talk about caring for your wildness, learning how to befriend it, and how it often gets into tangles with your strongly developed empathy and morals.

The wildness—the wild side of self—we're referring to comes from the unconscious place inside those with OCD that, as we've noted in previous chapters, needs to be named, tamed, and reframed. The empathic, moral side comes into play when we are trying to live up to what we say we hold dear. But what happens when these sides tussle? Is it possible to declare them both winners? We'll showcase how to deepen your connection to *both* your wild side *and* your empathic, moral side in the pages ahead.

FROM CONFLICT TO CREATIVE COLLABORATION

Why am I sharing so much about how the unconscious works in all its manifestations from dynamic repression (Freud's unconscious of conflicts and hidden motivations) to the normative unconscious (the universal unconscious)? Because I want you to get comfortable with it, to befriend it as we did those parts inside (remember good me, bad me, and not me?). I want to show you how helpful and useful the unconscious is, how it can move you from conflict to creative collaboration.

I hope you'll start to enjoy rather than fear how nuanced and rich the unconscious is, how many more subtle dimensions there are of getting to know your full experience, and how it can never, nor does it ever have to, be entirely pure, controlled, or defined. There is a solidity within the fluidity that you can trust. This is the wonder and beauty of the unconscious, and I invite you to approach your OCD as a manifestation of this dynamic, integrated, and nuanced creature instead of as a terrorizer that slides you into a seeming black hole of chaos and entropy.

The final value in learning how to roll with and benefit from integrating the unconscious is not only increased mindfulness, as is so popular these days, but also enhanced embodiment. We've seen and are well aware of how much those of us with OCD quickly gravitate to managing and processing nearly everything through our minds. When we forget and disconnect from our bodies—the wild side of not only darkness and depravity but also of instinct, feeling, and passion—we lose a side that can richly inform and enhance the depth and dimension of our humanity.

WHERE THE WILD THINGS ARE

From the start of our journey, I alluded to the quintessential wild child, Max, from the book *Where the Wild Things Are* (Sendak, 1984). His story is quite simple but emblematic of the universal struggle of living and taming the wild side of the unconscious. In the original version by Maurice Sendak, Max makes mischief of all sorts in his wolf suit, hammering up a makeshift fort in his bedroom that features a teddy bear hanging in effigy and menacingly running after his dog with a fork.

In the 2009 film version written by Spike Jonze and Dave Eggers, we learn new details of Max's backstory. Max is not only slightly older, a nine-year-old on the border between childhood and adolescence, but he is also the only son of a single mother. Like the Max of the original, this Max has a wild imagination and a profound sensitivity. He is painted as a lonely, misunderstood creature who is heartbroken when his teenage sister not only ignores his bids for connection but also abandons him when her teenage friends crush his snow igloo—with him inside of it—during a snowball fight.

Max's wildness in initiating the snowball fight is his primal way of connecting in a world that feels isolated and broken. It is a cry, even a yelp, for help. His sister's lack of response brings on a fit of rage and he runs upstairs to trash her room; he shakes the snow off of himself onto her bed and carpet and tears apart a heart decoration she made for their mother.

Max tries to alert his mother about his pain, loneliness, and confusion when she returns home. While she apologizes for his sister's bad behavior and attempts to tune into his sadness, she is taken away into her own land of confusion, trying to correct a project for work before she, too, gets in trouble.

Later, Max is again heartbroken to find that his mother is more interested in having dinner with her new boyfriend than spending special time with him. He stands on the kitchen island in his wolf costume and howls and then runs around the house chasing the dog with a fork, and, in response to his mother's scolding of his embarrassing behavior, he bites her on the shoulder (the "I'll eat you up" parallel to the Sendak version). Terrified of his own badness, he runs away into the woods. He then takes the journey on his sailboat to the place where the wild things are.

All of the elements of Jonze and Eggers's (2009) and Sendak's (1984) *Where the Wild Things Are* have relevance and resonance for those who struggle with OCD. Those with OCD are afflicted with a primal emotional sensitivity and awareness. Max himself is in tune with his own emotions but he is even more sensitized to the desire, fear, embarrassment, and confusion of his mother and sister. He is looking for companionship with these feelings, with these sides of himself, so that he can learn how to master, tame, and make a home for them that is more solid than the igloo he built.

Without that companionship, his feelings run wild. He bites his own mother and makes himself his own pariah by excommunicating himself from the suburban world that he's known all of his life.

As in Sendak's story, however, there is an innovative turn and transformation in the story. Max befriends the primal aspects of himself, the wild unconscious stuff that we're all made of, in the form of the wild things. And in so doing, he becomes a king and reconnects with the desire to come back home, with a new facet of himself joined in Kintsugi-style to an old one that was once abandoned.

THE WILDNESS OF MULTIPLE, COLLIDING TRUTHS

The wildness of your OCD will come in different forms. You might not notice it at first because it doesn't always conform to conventional shapes; and, as we've seen in prior chapters, it takes form both figuratively and literally. Your OCD might show its wild side by resisting a conventional path, by showcasing a feeling you find abhorrent (or at the very least have an emotionally allergic reaction to it), or by flaunting some aspect of yourself that feels so contradictory and wrong that it could never fit right.

OCD becomes both difficult and illuminating because it forces you to tolerate and become more open to multiple and contradictory truths, to recognize how powerfully and intensely humans can feel love and hate simultaneously. How is it possible that love and hate can coexist in such nuanced and complex ways? How is it possible to hold firm to boundaries so that individuality is possible and yet connection can be close at hand too? These are the intricate questions that OCD attempts to ask and answer—but not without an internal fight.

In this chapter, we will look at cases in which this fight happens—from conflicts around one's work life, identity, and capacity for goodness to the nature of marriage and sustaining self and other in relationship, and to facing the ultimate conflict of life and death in one's own body and mind.

THE CONVENTIONAL WILD SIDE

Former child actress and author Mara Wilson (2016) shares a quintessential story in her memoir about the ways in which OCD censors and inhibits the conventional wild sides, flooding the self with shame, worry, and doubt. In a chapter titled "The Junior Anti-Sex League," we learn about Wilson's development as a young crusader against the dangers and wrongness of sex.

At the close of the chapter is a scene at a weekend sleepaway camp where Wilson innocently experiments with the beginnings of sexuality, playing games like *Truth or Dare?*, *Kill/Marry/Screw*, and *Spin the Bottle*. When she and her friends are caught and censured by the camp counselor, she feels enormous guilt, especially when, on the ride home from camp, her father—who is unaware of her recent transgressions—comments on his pride in her successful return from an overnight, "You did a good thing this weekend, Mara!" (Wilson, 2016, p. 29).

Internally branding herself a "casual kisser" who wouldn't even remember or even know who her first kiss was, Wilson soon recognizes that she has found something new that is more "fun than being judgmental." A realization about the OCD fiction begins to dawn on her:

"I think I'd always be able to control my impulses. I thought I could outsmart my instincts. If I were just bright enough and disciplined enough, I thought, I could outwit basic human biology. But I had felt it as much as everyone else there, if not more" (p. 29).

Wilson gets at what we so often see, as did Freud early on with many of his Victorian cases including with the Ratman: the tormenting inner conflict of the mind against its own body. The conflict shows up most floridly and dramatically in those with OCD because their minds are so exquisitely moral, self-aware, and self-conscious that they give rise to the most intricate ways of attempting to control—by sheer force of will—what Wilson describes as basic human biology. That wonderfully expansive mind can be our own worst enemy, as well, when it comes to the matters of the body and the heart.

The reason all OCD sufferers need to come into more compassionate connection to their wild side is because it is so very human and cannot, as some falsely believe, be controlled and outwitted. It is fundamental, instinctual, and, as Freud has tried to show, the essence of healthy pleasure too. In the end, every OCD sufferer must come to Wilson's droll conclusion: "Every moralist is a hypocrite" (Wilson, 2016, p. 29). In being with and living through this nuanced contradiction, one finds an entirely different integration in a wholly new club worth joining.

WALKING ON THE WILD SIDE

In his 2022 memoir, *Harder to Breathe*, founding drummer for Maroon 5 and now-therapist Ryan Dusick chronicles the surprising journey he took leaving the wild side of a rock star life to heal his anxiety, depression, and alcoholism. Dusick (2022) notes that his perfectionism reached an unsustainable crescendo and that playing more than five hundred shows a year to bring the fledgling band success with their first album took an exacting toll. Speaking through his own body, his psyche literally shut down his capacity to play drums as a message that he needed to reclaim the hidden wild side he wasn't listening to: the wild side that goes against convention and is clamoring to be heard and given shelter. He credits his "nervous breakdown" and the musical dystonia (a neurological condition that affects the production of music) that emerged from this as a turning point not just in his career but also in how he viewed life itself. As we'll see below, this wild side is an inside job, and many people, especially those with OCD, fail to recognize it.

As a culture, happily, we are seeing more care for this wildness in stories of high-level performers like Simone Biles and Naomi Osaka, and this is changing the dialogue about prioritizing this internal world. Now a mental health advocate for the general public and especially for those in the performing arts, athletics, and public eye, Dusick champions a more integrated way of living and working, one that showcases the kind of caring for our wildness that we'll be working on here.

WHEN THE PERP IS YOU

Sean's friends and family didn't get it. Just as his career as an actor was beginning to take off, he decided to take a break. Really to take a stand. Although he was playing secondary characters on television, he was making it on big-time stuff. He found a successful niche playing the perpetrator you least likely suspect on network television shows like *Chicago PD* and *CSI*.

But something was wrong, and his psyche knew it. Like Dusick's perfectionistic nagging, Sean had always felt that he had to perform, especially when it came to doing what was conventional and correct. Like Lin-Manuel Miranda, whom he missed by a few years, Sean had graduated from Wesleyan University. He was prepped for both a conventional back-up career in law or his lifelong dream of being an actor. And he had done everything right, graduating on time despite setbacks with anxiety, being super responsible with an insurance policy back-up major, and, as always, being a charmingly connected student involved in loads of altruistic extracurriculars.

But just as Ryan Dusick found his hands and arms not working to do the drumming he was born to do, Sean found himself throwing auditions. And it totally baffled him.

For a perfectionist who feels that his safety and stability ride on pleasing others—like his family, the culture, or his own internal moral compass—the wild side can come in a seemingly mundane form. Like a decision to leave his job and do something completely unexpected.

The wild side that gets lost in OCD doesn't always map to the wild side you typically expect. We know the OCD that tortures the sufferer with concerns of being a pedophile, psychopath, or some other conventional monster. But in its true, sleight-of-hand way, OCD can also arrive in the form of what might not stick out as obviously wild but *feels* wild on the inside, nonetheless.

"I've pushed through the door into Hollywood like a total badass but all I want is to have a normal nine to five, so I have time to read and play my guitar whenever I want."

Not surprisingly, Sean's parents and friends were up in arms about his decision, and they begged him to do the right thing. What they didn't understand was that Sean needed to have the freedom and choice to rebel in the ways that were right for *him*.

For a clue as to how Sean's psyche was trying to alert him to this dilemma, recall the characters Sean was always drawn to and, not surprisingly, what directors saw as most alive in him. Sean was always the perpetrator, the one you least suspected, but the one, in the end, who did it. It was no psychological coincidence that Sean gravitated toward these roles. It was the way his psyche was trying to communicate his need for more balance in tending to and living in his wild side.

And this wild side wasn't literally being a criminal at all. Living in his wild side meant being a bit of a rebel and a bit of an asshole in relation to what everyone in his culture felt he should be doing and in all that he internalized. He didn't need to be a triple threat in order to be valuable, and he didn't need to have only his goodness as a star student. He needed to be with his own wildness.

And this wildness was Sean's freedom to trust that his inner needs were more important than the outer pressures, just as Ryan Dusick eventually found in his journey. It was unexpected even for Sean to decode that his wild side was exactly the opposite of what most people thought of as the wild side, and yet it was essential for him to heal and grow. Most importantly, without a sense of wildness, Sean did not have the motivation or vitality to do anything, and it began to show itself in deepening depression. When the anxiety signals of OCD are not working, the next messenger is secondary depression.

Although this depression, at first blush, may appear to be problematic and merely exacerbating the torture, a quote often attributed to Carl Jung (source unknown) reminds us that it is something extremely positive and helpful for more all-encompassing growth: "Depression is like a woman in black. If she turns up, don't shoo her away. Invite her in, offer her a seat, treat her like a guest and listen to what she wants to say."

Sean needed my help noticing and shining a light on his wild side and making room for it so he could be more fully himself. The moral side that tugged at him from the opposite direction compelled him to do all that was expected of him, all that's good and right about the world. This moral side was *not* in his full self-interest without his wild side too. We incorporated both in a more nuanced way to set him free.

Not only did Sean's symptoms abate but he also started to feel more spontaneous interest in figuring out his career from the inside-out. And ironically enough, he didn't stop acting, instead, he no longer had to solely focus on being the perp. Case closed.

MARRYING THE WRONG PERSON

It was the last place he wanted his OCD to flare up. On his honeymoon in the unrivaled beauty of the islands of Micronesia, he couldn't shake it this time. Relationship OCD, the insidious fear and doubt that his romantic partner wasn't the right match was in full effect.

Like so many with OCD, Andrew didn't understand what was wrong with him. Why couldn't he enjoy the romantic dinners overlooking the turquoise waters framed by sculptured volcanic mountains and look into his new wife's stunningly mysterious hazel eyes? And yet all he could think of was whether his wife was as good as his last girlfriend who had broken things off, or worse yet, of that intriguing woman he met in the lobby of the hotel with whom he struck up a lively conversation.

His head was swirling with anxiety. It was crazy. Even the very fact that he was doubting this on his own honeymoon seemed to be a sign that it was all wrong. He had made a mistake and now he would hurt this woman he thought he loved. How would he tell her? How would he tell his own family and all the people who had showered them with celebration and gifts?

Andrew's guilt intensified with every moment of seeming joy with his new wife. When they were hiking on a trail to a magnificent waterfall or snorkeling together amid a rainbow sea of fish, he felt more and more like a sham. How could he be so heartless and such a fool?

Fresh off an anxiety bender one evening, he chanced upon an article in the *New York Times* with an intriguing and almost synchronistic title: "Why You Will Marry the Wrong Person." Written by author and philosopher of everyday life Alain de Botton (2016), the piece was instantly consoling in the best way possible. Contrary to what you might think, it wasn't compulsive reassurance operating here but finally an acknowledgement of Andrew's wild side.

According to De Botton, it is nearly inevitable for any of us to marry the right person, and is simplistic and naive to believe there won't be complications. Because of the shift in culture away from marrying for economic, religious, or social reasons, more and more people are choosing love as their north star. However, this same freedom comes with the increasing pressure for one person to function as your everything. To make matters worse, most people aren't fully known until they are knee-deep in a committed relationship (and love can't completely save you then) and also seek familiarity that is both good and bad for both persons in the relationship. In short, relationships, like the psyche itself, are much more complex, nuanced, and messy than we all wish them to be.

Andrew was heartened to find that his existential dilemmas weren't so absurd, far-fetched, or problematic. It was right on target for someone just entering, and now celebrating, marriage.

As Puck from *A Midsummer Night's Dream* says, "What fools these mortals [in love] be!" (Shakespeare, 2015), and how silly it is for us to feel like we can be in full control of and certain about our partners. In many ways, accepting the wild truth that it isn't possible to comfortably carry this is important for all of us, but especially those with relationship OCD. De Botton reminds us of how quick we are to unfairly frame ourselves on this point, as if it were anything but normal.

The wild side comes not just in impulsively trusting our passions and leaving our mate to paint women in Tahiti like Paul Gaugin, it comes in recognizing that there is a wildness in being able to be with the messy, difficult, complicated challenge of being so close to another flawed and perfectly imperfect human being. This is the wild side that Andrew needed to enjoy his trip, find his center, and begin the new chapter of his happily complicated life.

TOM AND THE BUTTERFLY

It all began after a playful fight among friends over who-knows-what. Was it the foul that wasn't called in the basketball game moments before or some long-simmering resentment among these two fourteen-year-old boys who had seemed inseparable since childhood? It didn't really matter because, from that day forward, my patient Tom was obsessed. An innocent blow to the head was now a rumination set in motion, and from that day forward, nobody could touch him or else he'd be dead.

Such is the way OCD strikes. It's almost always about the loss of someone we love or our own very precious, fragile, and meaningful life. And it's almost always about a black-and-white choice of living or dying, having or losing, and never shall the two ever meet again (more on that in the next chapter).

I was working with Tom to recognize just how quickly he cut himself off at the neck, using his *gifted* and imaginative mind to control and negotiate all that was happening in the real estate underneath that he so often neglected. We were working on tracking Tom's hidden wild side.

"There's a body down there with a fuller story, and we need to get that part working with your mind as the best friends they're truly meant to be. Let's see if we can get his version out there on the table and have them coexist."

It was an unusual request. To see the body and the mind, both such seemingly opposite and antagonistic sides, as allies and compatriots was a revelation. He sat there intrigued yet skeptical: "Yeah, what can my body do for me? Didn't it already get me in trouble with that fight?"

"Of course, it seems that way on the surface, but psychological growth is almost always at the intersection of your mind and body," I said. "Maybe we just need to get to know your body better and trust its counsel too."

So we worked on giving Tom's body a voice, and it talked about its own desire to be more confident and *assertive*, even tough. But the mind didn't like this because it meant there might be "messy" run-ins, someone might get hurt, and then the game felt like it would all be over. Those ambivalences weren't easy to sit with, no less to reconcile.

"Yeah, but maybe we can allow both of these to be there together so we can find a third option. The creative process is always about transforming, yet it feels a lot like destruction at first," I said.

Tom's mind perked up while his body knew everything in his bones. Life was messier and muddier and for someone with Tom's sensitivity that wasn't always easy to bear, but at least now he had someone like me to help him carry it. It didn't feel as scary as being alone in his philosophical mind trying to reconcile life and death at every turn.

He practiced trusting in his body just a little bit more each session. We joked about how challenging it is to be human like this, to allow ourselves to have our own space and others to have it too, and yet to find ways of making true contact. There always seemed to be some stepping on toes or bumping into each other as we attempted to make deeper connections. But Tom was allowing it to be okay, he was obsessing less about his head and noticing more in his heart. "Maybe it's just our own human way of chasing our own tails," Tom told me presciently. He was getting it!

Tom was allowing himself change while being the same, but he still wondered about where the center held. He was feeling more open, relaxed, and zen-like about keeping both straight, but sometimes he wondered if he was really losing himself, maybe even the best part of himself. His mind was the strongest and most reliable side of him. He worried that the wild side of his feelings and body would lead him astray.

I reminded him of the plight and beauty of the caterpillar who knows he is changing too. It doesn't feel fair to leave that crawling body, and its many prolegs lose all power and control. But I marveled at him with a picture of the glorious wings of the monarch butterfly. "You are changing forms but staying the same, our most difficult but essential trick. Look at what's in the middle of this butterfly?" And he saw it. Smack at the center was the caterpillar form anchoring and centering the butterfly itself. "This is the strange balancing act of gaining and losing and finding that new creative discovery."

Tom wanted to understand how this connected to the exposure and response prevention (ERP) skills he had learned in prior therapy.

"Am I avoiding my anxiety and just getting reassurance from you about this?"

I shook my head, smiling. "Actually, you're doing the deepest and most profound ERP of all. You're looking at the fundamental hope and grief we have about existing and potentially not-existing, you are holding the strange balance of holding and losing ourselves and each other all of the time. And you are integrating your body and mind, and that is making all of the difference."

The great neurologist Oliver Sacks (1990) recognizes that when "illness" changes us, we have to find a way to adapt it to our *identity*, and it becomes as much part of us as anything else. Similarly, OCD had become Tom's strategy for regulating his intensely sensitive nature and provided him with so much, and yet it also sometimes fought other new sides from coming online.

"So, now, I can still hold onto that OCD side like a friend even though at times it can be a bully?"

"Yes, we are taming that side so that it isn't such a bully and so it can collaborate with your body in ways that it can trust. It doesn't have to be a choice between life and death anymore or between either of these sides in you or in others. They can both become best friends again."

We had found Tom's unique wild side together. Tom was relieved, and together we marveled at the beauty that this butterfly might miss out on if it didn't fulfill its mission of flying and pollinating all of the flowers that make up this wonderful world. How funny it was, we joked together, that the answer was right there in front of us in nature all along, staring us both right in the face.

THE WILD UNCONSCIOUS BRINGS IT ALL TOGETHER

Why are all these wild sides so important? And why are they so intimately connected to the unconscious that I introduced with Weinberger's research? When OCD treatment moved from talk therapy to cognitive behavioral approaches, it held on to an important aspect of its radical behaviorist philosophy that what cannot be seen and measured isn't worth focusing on. Happily, the research of Weinberger and others is demonstrating that the unconscious can be studied and measured. It's about time it can be integrated into a fuller understanding of how and why OCD operates the way it does.

As you notice by the case studies above, the unconscious side can only be understood in the individual's social-emotional context. It can only be seen in the light of relationships. This is one of the great limitations and drawbacks of a purely cognitive behavioral approach. It presumes that OCD behavior is operating in a relational vacuum.

In the behavioral view, OCD occurs purely because of negative reinforcement—that is, avoidance behavior strengthens the obsessions and/or compulsions, and context has no bearing whatsoever on this. In the cognitive view, the OCD mind is like a computer that only needs to be debugged and reprogrammed. In their view, the only contribution that relationships bring to the OCD sufferer is to help them work on treatment. There is no indication that they have any possible impact on the emotional context of the OCD sufferer's environment at all. It is as if the OCD sufferer is merely a computer without human sentience.

Both conceptions have the social and emotional context—part of what makes us so very human—drop out. Without this important information about the wild unconscious, as I've termed it, you have a highly impoverished and simplistic version of OCD.

The dimension that the wild unconscious brings to OCD is immeasurable and, like Weinberger's research on elections, it can also be quite unexpected. Who would have expected the perp to be you or that you'd marry the wrong person? A simplistic reading of these statements misses the nuance that makes them so interesting, personal, and worthy of full integration. It's for this reason, as Mary Oliver suggested at the beginning of this chapter, that we need to continually ask, *What will you, as an OCD sufferer, do with this one wild and precious life?*

EXERCISES: CARING FOR YOUR WILDNESS

Rockwell-Evans (2023) notes that one of the main, and most misguided, rules imposed by OCD is that you should be in control at all times. Not surprisingly, this control comes from your mind at the expense of your problematic, immoral, and dangerous body. In this exercise, I'd like to reframe your wildness as having wisdom all its own, noticing the ways it attempts to add dimension and complexity to aspects of yourself and relationships.

The first step is to notice this wild side. Are you a "moralist that's also a hypocrite" like Mara Wilson? "Is the perp you" as in the case of Sean? Have you married the wrong person as Allain de Botton suggests? Or are you just afraid of the changes entailed in becoming a butterfly like Tom?

The controlling mind and harsh conscience want to have little to do with this instinctual, wild creature. This side of you is much like Paul Rudd's character, Peter Klaven, in the movie *I Love You Man* (Hamburg, 2009) a soon-to-be-married guy with no significant male friend to call upon to be his best man.

Peter meets Jason Segal's character, Sidney Fife, who is unabashedly connected to his wild side, shown in his willingness to confront former Hulk star Lou Ferigno, his rock star drumming, and his willingness to take risks and do seemingly wrong things (like enjoying the free food and picking up divorced women at high-end real estate showings). Over time, however, Peter learns how to appreciate the liveliness he's been missing out on with this side and how much of a truly good person and friend Sidney can be even through his wild side, too.

Let's play with how this wild side might be giving you something valuable even if it seems to contaminate or corrupt your vision. Does it allow you to showcase other facets of your emotional world, your anger, your sexuality, your fatigue (remember Ryan Dusick?), or even just the fear of change itself?

Remember that your wild side doesn't even have to fit the conventional definition of "wild," it is primarily about rebelling against what it feels like you *should* be doing.

What do you feel like you should be doing and who said you can't be or explore these other sides? Remind yourself that they are not all of you, just facets of the fluid self (or selves), the multitudes, to echo Walt Whitman, that we are all trying to contain and express.

6

MAKING MEANING
IN THE FACE OF DEATH

There's a common misconception about OCD that it's an anxiety about everything under the sun; it depends merely on the day to determine how the sun distorts the world for one particular OCD sufferer versus another. The infinite variety of OCD presentations makes it easy to forget that among the many subtypes—contamination, harm, responsibility, relationship, health OCD, and so on—something unifies it. Or rather something much bigger, as we'll shortly learn.

It's a secret hidden in plain sight. And most OCD sufferers can tell you quite nonchalantly if you just ask them. One interviewer presumed that record producer, musician, and singer Jack Antonoff's anxiety escalated due to the stress and wear-and-tear of being on tour. Antonoff (Weiss, 2015) surprised him with a virtual master class in what OCD is really about, saying: "It's not anxiety like stage fright or about doing a good job. It's strictly about mortality and health and my own existence. So, whether I'm singing in a band or just sitting on my couch I struggle either way. Actually, sometimes touring helps— there's a nice routine to it" (para. 14).

Surprise, surprise. To echo Weinberger's Seinfeldian moment in the previous chapter, the anxiety at the core of OCD isn't about just anything. It's about that *one* big thing: death. Freud was hip to this as far back as 1909 in his case of the Ratman. Listen in on his analysis of a potential unifying source for his OCD patients: "Their thoughts are increasingly occupied with other people's length of life and possibility of death; their superstitious propensities have had no other content to begin with and have perhaps no other source whatsoever" (Freud, 1963, p. 70).

Author and anxiety whisperer Sara Wilson puts it even more poetically, noting the intimate connection between anxiety and existential curiosity, the desire to understand what is bigger about ourselves and the world, and how easy it is to lose hold of this mystical connection in everyday life. Here's how Wilson first experienced that hidden secret:

> I touched a still, settled, vast, spacious, magnificent knowing at my core. It was only for a few delicate moments but there was no going back. The scab was removed and the rawness—the "Something Else" I'd been looking for—was finally exposed. I call it the Something Else because there's no other way of describing this yearning—this indescribable thing or place or energy I'd been looking for—that came before words. (2019, p. 43)

Wilson contends, like I do in this book, that the anxiety that we so quickly label as a problem is actually a disconnection from this "Something Else," the mystery of what might be bigger than death and yet can only be faced in confronting death itself.

> It's this lack of connection and clarity that leaves us fretting and checking and spinning around in our heads and needing to compensate with irrational painful behaviors, whether it be OCD, phobias, or panic attacks. It's this sense of *missing* . . . something . . . that leaves you feeling lonely and incomplete and fluttery. Something is not right. . . . I'm really fretting that something is missing that should be making me feel supported, comforted and assured that everything's going to be ok. (p. 45)

In an interview with author of *The Joy Thief: How OCD Steals Your Happiness and How to Get It Back,* Joy Moodie (2023), OCD expert Jonathan Grayson (*Women's Agenda,* 2023) muses on OCD's existential underpinnings:

> I think OCD is, in some sense, a philosophical disorder. Most of the concerns that people have are the great questions philosophers ask. "How can I be safe in a world where my family and I could die at any moment? What is the evil in me? What is the nature of God? Who am I?" And the only difference between somebody who has OCD and a great philosopher? "There's only one difference. People with OCD actually want an answer." (para. 16)

It's a wry but telling assertion about the nature of OCD that few have spent much time on. Perhaps out of fear that engaging it too deeply will degenerate into those thought spirals and keep OCD sufferers away from "living their values." But what if their values are in asking and attempting to answer these very questions? What if they have been asking them from the very beginning?

CONFRONTING THE CONCEPT OF DEATH

Remember painter Cristi López whose OCD fears began with her terror of sleepwalking with scissors? When Cristi was opening a show featuring her art's commentary on OCD, I talked with her about this not-so-hidden secret about OCD and death.

"Death, to me," I told her,

> is the root note of OCD. It's as if people with OCD have this capacity to notice the fragility of life and the possibility of death in a way that's much more intense than most. In its worst moments, it is the most harrowing part of OCD, and yet it can also imbue the world with quite a bit of meaning and dimension. I noticed that connection to death in your work as well. Cristi, you have this

wonderful painting called "Body Count." From the name, you'd think it'd be pretty gruesome, but instead, it's this interesting collection of women's faces being held by a central nude figure. They seem proud, strong, and vulnerable, and you can almost imagine them as multiple aspects of the main figure or the lovers she has kept. Echoing in the background of this lively picture is the pun of death.

López responded almost immediately, as if we had both been in on the secret from the start: "Death is the universal obsession. The undeniability of death is essentially the only thing that someone with OCD can accept as true. It's the only absolute. What easier thing is there to obsess over than something that you know is going to happen? All of my most troubling obsessions ultimately end in death, and my most fervent subjects of research are also death related."

Author Mara Wilson (2016) reminds us of the OCD sufferer's precocious attention to death and mortality. Just as Greta Thunberg was horrified by the plastic suffocating the lives of so many animals shown in documentaries, Wilson was haunted as a child by an astronomer ginning up the dangers of solar flares in order to capture the excitement of her and her fellow kindergarteners. Just as she imagined fire raining down and overtaking our helpless planet, the astronomer upped the ante by talking about all the ways the planet Venus could kill a human being. Wilson broke down in tears while her other classmates seemed unperturbed, wondering, "Am I the only one who understands?"

That phrase sums it up perfectly. It isn't that other people don't understand the enormity of mortality, it's that those with OCD have an unusually keen sense about these existential questions. Their expansive minds and generous hearts wonder and worry about these issues far too easily and early. It's no surprise then that, as a little girl, Wilson planned her funeral before her own wedding or that, at age five, she told her baby sister that everybody dies to prevent her from going through the same shock that she herself experienced upon first registering this terrifying truth.

This enhanced existential sensitivity doesn't feel like such a gift. Without the adult tools and emotional machinery to make sense of it all, this capacity to see death so soon feels like a curse. Or as Wilson wryly puts it: "If this is what it is to be special, it's terrible!"

FACING DEATH IN REAL LIFE

The fear of death not only haunts people with OCD in the abstract but it also occurs through a real-time experience with death itself. Termed a "boundary experience," this is an existential moment when we confront the limits of our existence. Shala Nicely was four years old and on her way to feed the ducks when her and her parents were struck by a car. From that day, her brain had to protect her from all of the dangers lurking in the newly broken world (Begley, 2018).

Nicely began to suffer from nightmares of her parents lying on a guillotine with moments to spare before the blade fell. When she awoke, the only thing that could save them—in her mind—was a devoted focus on the image of a chevalier racing to their rescue. Thus began a series of compulsions that morphed into counting in fours, checking that she hadn't mistakenly run over someone with her car, and, most eccentric and far-fetched of them all, making sure she didn't accidentally leave her cat Fred in the refrigerator (Nicely, 2018).

You might also remember this boundary experience with Ava Holmes, John Green's protagonist in *Turtles All the Way Down* (Green, 2017). Her father's unexpected heart attack and death activates her concerns about her own solidity and authority. If there was radar to find her OCD origin story, the event would light up from space. And not only is Ava on the hunt to solve the mysterious disappearance of fugitive billionaire Russel Pickett but she unknowingly tips us off to the existential core of OCD. In a poignant moment shared with her love interest, we spy a tender confession at the heart of OCD, bobbled back and forth between them: "When you lose someone, you realize you'll lose everyone. And once you know, you can never forget it (Green, 2017, p. 81).

The never-ending spiral of Ava's thoughts about life and death are ultimately balanced by the comical story of the woman who questions a scientist giving a detailed history of the earth and life on it. The woman shares that the entire world is resting on the back of a giant turtle. When the scientist questions her about what that turtle is standing on, she replies, "It's on another." When he gets flummoxed about what that turtle is on, she replies, "Sir, you don't understand. It's turtles all the way down" (p. 245).

KAFA'S LIVING NIGHTMARES

In addition to the concept of death in the abstract and in reality, there's another haunting form of death that is the psychological death of the self—meaning, the impossibility of having the space to be oneself and the pressure of being trapped inside a living nightmare. Nowhere could this form of psychic death be better illustrated than in the life and work of Franz Kafka.

Although he wasn't diagnosed with OCD (nor was it a formal diagnosis yet) and there's wide speculation of a host of other disorders he might have suffered from—clinical depression, schizoid personality, borderline personality, and possibly an atypical eating disorder—there's something about the thought process and disposition of Kafka, like Freud's Ratman, that bears significant parallels. Kafka (Fichter, 1988; Felisati & Sperati, 2005) tapped into and struggled with his existential sensitivity and the profound ambivalence that comes with being unable to answer the great philosophical questions. Like so many with OCD, he was severely misunderstood by both his family and his culture, and his profound sensitivity was seen less as a virtue than as a problem that he could only really work through alone at night in his writing and imagination. Other than his creativity, there was little to help him emotionally through his suffering.

Raised by a domineering and physically imposing father, Kafka grew up in a middle-class house in which material comfort and social advancement were idolized. He identified more with his maternal-side ancestors who were well-versed in spirituality and rabbinical literature, and who seemed, like him, to show a sensitive and melancholic disposition. Many of his stories focus on characters who, despite trying to exercise their own free will, are trapped and oppressed in a world that finds novel ways of dehumanizing them. Kafka found a kind of redemption in his late-night writings, which he produced parallel to his day job at an insurance agency, but his keen sensitivity and humanity were never fully honored or valued by his family (Fichter, 1988; Felisati & Sperati, 2005).

The characters in so many of Kafka's stories, from *The Metamorphosis* to *The Trial*, are tormented by the alienating world that the industrial revolution ushers in and are crushed by the lack of an authoritative voice to advocate for their subjective experiences. They were much like Kafka, who felt like his own literary ambitions were a distraction from what was truly important to his family.

Even though Kafka was finding his own voice as a writer just as psychotherapy itself was finding its voice—and its start with the work of Freud and others—he never believed or trusted in the power of therapy. He not only felt that it was impossible to answer those burning philosophical questions or exorcize his demons, but he also felt that working through them might actually extinguish the flames of his creativity and artistry. I sometimes wonder what might have happened if Kafka had ever learned of why and how his sensitivity was being overrun by so many impersonal and insensitive influences—both in his family and culture—and how his plight might have been healed both in his imaginative writing and in everyday life.

Although we'll never know, there's another brief story about Kafka that might give us some indication of the tenderness and thoughtfulness he might have brought to therapeutic work. And even this story itself is mysterious and perhaps merely apocryphal (Macguill, 2021).

The story goes that at the age of forty, Kafka was strolling in a park in Berlin when he came upon a little girl crying because she had lost her favorite doll. Together, they searched and searched for it to no avail. In order to console the girl, Kafka composed letters from the doll, chronicling her exciting adventures around the world. Eventually, he brings the little girl a new doll that he attempts to pass off as the original. After his death, the little girl, who was now grown into a woman, found a note hidden inside the doll that read: "Everything you love will probably be lost, but in the end, love will return in another way" (Maguill, 2021, para. 5).

We'll never know how Kafka might have been transformed himself if he had more of this love returned his way, or had his sensitivity been viewed for the true gift it was. We can be thankful for him for showcasing the depths of despair, alienation, and disconnection that occurs when the most intensely existential questions are asked in the most personal and immediate of ways, and there is no personal help to return them back like that lost doll.

SIX DEGREES OF KEVIN BACON

Many OCD sufferers feel misunderstood because current treatments fail to see the existential drama hidden in nearly all of its manifestations. They miss the emotional core, the "Kevin Bacon" found in six degrees or fewer.

Remember that old game you used to play as a kid? One person picks an actor—say, Julie Andrews. She was in the movie *Enchanted* with Amy Adams, who, in turn, was in *Night at the Museum 2* with Ben Stiller. Stiller was in *Meet the Parents* with Robert De Niro, who was also with Kevin Bacon in the movie *Sleepers*. Just a few steps—here, only four—and you're back to Kevin Bacon himself.

The core of OCD—our "Kevin Bacon"—is the fear of death and loss. Uniting a wide variety of OCD presentations—health obsessions, relationship insecurities, contamination fears, checking concerns—is a fundamental anxiety about the loss of our most precious gift: life and the relationships that sustain life itself. This is the root note formed by the triad of chaos, powerlessness, and fear that morphs into OCD.

THE EMOTIONAL CORE OF OCD: EXISTENTIAL SENSITIVITY

Many can track back their main preoccupations of OCD to this "Kevin Bacon" and, yet, nearly all OCD treatments fail to acknowledge the profound empathy and sensitivity behind it; nor do they see it as a potential strength. Instead, they label it distorted noise that's better tuned out.

OCD develops because of this profound sensitivity that goes untended and misunderstood. The good news is that it's quite easy to bring down OCD fears by witnessing and clarifying them rather than relegating them to mere *thoughts*, veritable tics of the mind to be managed rather than lovingly integrated into one's story. This is the emotional core—the "Kevin Bacon"—so easily missed by many OCD treatments today.

Let's take a moment to see how close nearly all of the OCD subtypes are to the "Kevin Bacon" of existential dread. Harm OCD is a rather easy one. Whether you're concerned about mistakenly driving over somebody in a hit-and-run or the accidental possibility of grabbing a knife from the kitchen drawer and impulsively stabbing your own child, these OCD fears are based in the existential dread that death is possible and that you could be its instigator.

Checking OCD also fits in this category. Some checkers get nervous that they might have left the stove on or a door unlocked with the ultimate consequence being the death of their loved ones, and that they were just one preventive step away from death, rather than, say, the harm OCD who imagines themselves as the direct agent.

Health OCD—the concern that one might contract, or might already have, a terrible virus or might transmit it to somebody else who is beloved—is a concern about the possible contagion of sickness that will lead to death. Again, it is a feature of the uncertainty and unpredictability of death that drives this particular subtype.

Relationship OCD might seem less directly linked, but it is only a few steps away. Because if you think about it, our attachments are one of the primary ways in which we feel safe and secure and have emotionally and physically survived for millennia. And in a world where extended family and community is eroding, there's even more pressure for our romantic relationships to serve these crucial survival needs protecting us from possible death and its social equivalent: rejection.

Even classic contamination OCD bears some peripheral features of worries about death. The disgust and dis-ease that one feels stems from the possibility that things are dirty and can never be clean or pure enough, and that it's only a matter of time before everything is destroyed with the filth that is symbolic of death.

As we've seen in prior chapters, OCD attempts to keep us fairly distracted and off the trail of these core feelings. And the existential core of it is just a deeper extension of everything we've been tracking. Getting in touch with the potential destructive feelings of hate, anger, sadness, and fear—to name a few—is difficult to do without feeling overwhelmed. Just as some of these precocious children with their existential OCD concerns—recall Mara Wilson, Greta Thunberg, or Cristi López—didn't have the emotional and cognitive wherewithal to absorb and fathom the terrifying concerns the world presented, even adults struggle to be with the awe-inspiring bigness of that "Something Else" (Wilson, 2019).

But being able to source all of these OCD concerns to a unified place can provide a sense of relief, order, and possibility. If those with OCD are like great philosophers, maybe they just need a little more credit given for how much they can perceive, how early they can receive it, and how they can make form out of it.

Mara Wilson (2016) confesses at the start of her memoir that both through her acting in such movies as *Mrs. Doubtfire* and *Matilda*, but even more so in her life, she has always had the narrative need, the deeply human impulse to make a narrative tapestry out of all the disparate threads of her life.

In this next case, we'll explore how those threads are woven together using this existential material as a frame.

THE MANY DIMENSIONS OF DEATH

Ashley was in the midst of mourning the loss of her mother; she had always expected her to die young but never imagined it happening so soon. Ashley had OCD throughout her life in a variety of forms: checking stove handles and making sure the front door was locked, obsessional reviews to assure she didn't inadvertently say something hurtful to friends or family, and compulsively checking her high school and college papers for completely accurate reporting of statistics and even her own opinions.

It was no surprise to Ashley that she would be challenged by the stress and shock of her mother's death, but she also found it curious how many new kinds of OCD symptoms began to crop up. She could no longer write her name for fear of spelling out the word "Ash" and somehow tarnishing the honor of her mother who vehemently opposed cremation and wanted to be buried, as was customary in her religion. Ashley also began obsessing that minor aches and pains could be possible harbingers of her coming death, worrying that she might miss a sign that could help prevent her own untimely death.

Ashley noticed that many of these symptoms came up as she was working on cleaning up her mother's home—sorting through papers, making decisions about what to keep and junk. There were days that she worked for hours on end, forgetting to take breaks and have meals. And as she did, the OCD symptoms took their place, feeding her with courses and courses of doubts and fears.

She and I examined all of this from its "Kevin Bacon" existential center. It was crucial to give Ashley psychological room to put out all of her feelings and thoughts about her mother's death on the metaphorical table. The story was much deeper than the headline. Ashley's mother had been abusing alcohol for years and despite being able to hold down a job and keep the veneer of an ordinary life, she had been slowly killing herself.

Ashley was struggling to make sense of such a death and was wrestling with feelings of not just sadness but anger too. Why hadn't her mother listened to her and the many others who warned her? Why hadn't she been more sensitive to the burden this would put on Ashley, as the only child, picking up the pieces and literally taking on the settling of her mother's estate? Ashley thought it was selfish and cruel for her to feel this way, but it was an important part of the mixture of feelings she had. We could easily see how her OCD symptoms were trying to amplify and exaggerate these feelings—making her feel guilty for writing the word "Ash" to signal how fired up she was about how unfair and hurtful it all was—and then making her feel guilty for having those emotions in the first place.

Ashley began to totally disconnect from her body, skipping meals and working to exhaustion. Many of Ashley's OCD symptoms came up when she was tired, hungry, and totally disconnected from her body. I analogized her mind as trying to feed her with obsessions and compulsions instead of allowing her more compassionate and embodied connection. OCD served her snacks and junk food instead of nourishing meals.

As we began to make these links, it wasn't hard to understand why Ashley was also starting to feel concerns about her own mortality. The young age at which her mother passed made Ashley feel even more susceptible. In addition, the guilt she felt about her anger and frustration at her mother began to attack her in violent fears about being done in herself, almost as if in retribution for her own selfishness.

While Ashley's obsessions and compulsions seemed, at first, to be disconnected and wholly different from anything she had experienced in the past, the existential framework helped her to bring it all together. By having a safe space where she could make meaning in the face of death and ask all of these trying and painful questions in the presence of a supportive and empathic other, Ashley was able to fully decode OCD's existential core.

EXERCISE: IN WHAT WAY DOES DEATH COME FOR YOU?

Did death come for you in a precocious awareness like Cristi López, in a real-life scenario like Shala Nicely, or as the Kafkaesque combination of the impossibility of finding room in life and your imagination?

If it came from your being aware and sensitive to the concept of death, can you begin to have more empathy for how big, scary, and challenging it has been to carry without more emotional support?

Imagine for a moment a compassionate and kind adult being with you in your fears and anxieties about death in a way that normalizes, soothes, and creates room for finding a comforting understanding. Think of someone like Fred Rogers from *Mister Rogers' Neighborhood* or poet Emily Dickinson who describes sharing a hard truth like death "as lightning to the children / eased with explanation kind."

John Green's use of the metaphor of turtles all the way down is also a soothing image that moves from calamitous uncertainty to trust and faith that something is carrying what seems like it isn't being carried. The expression itself derives from Hindu mythology and is a way of alleviating the terror and fear of having no solid foundation. It envisions a structure that uses infinity to master concerns over precariousness.

FROM AWFUL TO AWESOME: TAPPING INTO GENERATIVE AWE

Can we transform the fear of death into a healthy exploration of what Sarah Wilson (2019) calls the "Something Else"? In flipping the terror of death, we start to explore and articulate the awe-someness of life.

There is much contemporary research on the power of awe. The upside of OCD helps us move from the terror and fear of death to the beauty and power of awe. Remember that the word "awe," as Dacher Keltner (2024) writes, comes from the root word of fear and terror. An essential task of OCD treatment is normalizing the enormity of emotion that comes with confronting existential truths and transforming them into the beauty found in awe.

In *Star Trek* (Roddenberry, 1966–1969), Captain Kirk, the fictional character that William Shatner played, helmed the *Starship Enterprise* with the mission to "boldly go where no man has gone before." However, when Shatner went up in space in real life, he had the reverse experience of hope and optimism. He felt the terrifying side of awe that is so often associated with OCD: the overwhelming awareness of death. As he said upon his return to Earth: "My trip to space was supposed to be a celebration; instead, it felt like a funeral. It was amongst the strongest feelings of grief I have ever encountered. The contrast between the vicious coldness of space and the warm nurturing of Earth below filled me with overwhelming sadness" (Lock, 2022, paras. 2 and 10).

This aspect of death and grief is akin to the feeling of chaos that underlies OCD. "Chaos" originated as a word to denote the abyss, the nothingness that preceded all creation. It is not only the antithesis of life itself but also returns us to the place before life even existed. So much of the overcompensated order and ritual of OCD are attempts to ward off the painful awareness found within death and before life and creation itself.

According to awe researcher Dacher Keltner, "Awe is the feeling of being in the presence of something vast that transcends your current understanding of the world" (2024, p. 7). The mystery within awe doesn't become one of painful or problematic uncertainty but, instead, becomes beautiful and inspiring. Keltner reminds us that it quiets "the nagging, self-critical, overbearing, status conscious voice of our self, or ego . . . empowering us to collaborate, to open our minds to wonder, and to see the deep patterns of life. . . . Awe brings us joy, meaning and commitment, along with healthier voices and more creative minds" (2024, p. xx).

Whether through the means of art, music, writing, or an intentional (and not OCD) ritual, we take the fear, terror, and chaos out of death by finding ways to honor it with sensitivity and love. We do this by recognizing the bigness of it that we can't fully encompass—just like we can't control every inch of the floor from contamination or our thoughts from their own wanderings—but that we can somehow make space for in our hearts and minds. In short, we can be in the presence of the vastness and mystery of it without having to solve it. It's like a deeper form of exposure and response prevention where we recognize that a form of faith allows that which we only partially know to be okay. In this openness, we touch some of the truths, all the while recognizing that we can't capture them all.

7

FREEING THE MUSE WITHIN THE CRITIC

Experimental psychologist and neuroscientist Ethan Kross (2021) studies the steady stream of voices in our heads. One research finding he's fond of sharing boasts a stunning conclusion: we talk to ourselves, internally, at a rate that is equivalent to speaking four thousand words per minute out loud. As he marvels, that's about 320 State of the Union addresses each day (Kross, 2021, p. xxii).

OCD leads you down rabbit holes of rumination and doubt—imagine 320 sadistic State of the Unions a day!—and yet, by learning to harness its constructive potential, you catch the critic in the act and find your way back to the muse. To do this well and consistently, we must understand just what the critic is and why it acts the way it does.

The critic is the devious and sinister inner voice that undermines, instead of illuminates, with its questions. It loves control and offers it for a steep price; you don't notice how much interest it expects from you in the fine print. Poet Linda Pastan (1998) characterizes the critic as a jail warden that locks us in or out. "No matter what voice they choose, or what language they speak" the messages are always the same: "Why can't you do anything right" and "We just don't love you anymore" (Pastan,1998, p. 244).

Psychologist Donald Kalsched (1996), in his book *The Inner World of Trauma*, highlights a more complex portrait of this inner terrorizer. While it undermines and harasses you, it's also a protective figure—think lion that guards your door and then turns on you when you open it to the world—ensuring that trauma doesn't recur and your spirit is kept alive. The critic functions as a survival mechanism when the world or environment is not safe enough to take creative risks. Over time, this protective structure takes on a life of its own forming what Kalsched (1996) calls the "self-care system."

The critic becomes the part of self that cuts off and dissociates from potential harm as it simultaneously disconnects from new possible life. It hermetically seals you in your overactive head and scrambles the signal for integrating your mind with your body. It creates a nightmarish world that only it can lord over and uses potential signals of perceived danger to press its case that it is the only one equipped to keep you intact.

The critic strikes at the point of deep pain, but it does so in a way that inflicts even more pain. We see the critic embodied in the character Iago from Shakespeare's *Othello* (Shakespeare, 2015). Iago is well aware that, deep in his heart, Othello feels insecure as a Moor about to marry Desdemona, the white daughter of an aristocratic senator. And Iago knows how to sow the seeds of doubt in Othello's mind by merely hinting at Desdemona's possible infidelity and doing so in an elaborate ruse involving the first gift given to her by Othello himself: a handkerchief. And we all know that, like most Shakespearian tragedies, what follows becomes Othello's total unravelling.

The critic is both a trap and a soother. It provides the rationale to keep fearing and warding off the most difficult and unimaginable of horrors, the loss of true love, the destruction of the self, and exile from community. But as we know from psychotherapy, the critic, like OCD itself, can be tamed, humanized, and tempered and brought into service of what is good and real.

OCD advocate Ethan Smith (personal communication, December 5, 2023) likes to say that through recovery he has found a way to use OCD's creativity for good instead of evil. And such is the focus of the chapter ahead: to showcase why and how you can transform what begins as the OCD critic into the muse for potential growth, connection, and integration.

More specifically, the OCD critic has a few common targets in its sights that are worth identifying so we know what it is trying to attack and how not to fall prey to its common lies and fearmongering, which attempt to have *you* submit to it rather than take new risks. First, the OCD critic will put down, minimize, and devalue your exquisite emotional and empathic sensitivity and try to sell it to you as a weakness and deficiency: "If only you were more like others, with less tuned-in brains and hearts, you'd be worthy and functional. But look at you, you're just a mess!" See how quickly and easily it can get inside of you?

Second, the OCD critic won't tolerate the fire in your anger and disagreement. It doesn't believe that you can be assertive without also being guilty, selfish, and/or destructive. It thinks this of even your healthy hate—that is, the rightful frustration we all, as human beings, experience when an important objective or feeling is blocked. Such fire is dangerous and problematic according to the OCD critic.

Third, the OCD critic minimizes, denies, and devalues your profound sensitivity to issues of life and death: the existential ground of our human universe. It mocks it as being overblown that you even notice how precious and fragile the human ecosystem is or how miraculous it is when we actually respect and honor that balance. This critic likes to make you feel badly about how sensitive you are to this and demands you to move beyond being so pathetically human.

What are the kinds of traumas that install the critic and its self-care system in the first place? Throughout these pages, we've seen countless examples, but here I'll boil them down to three distinct kinds: (1) real-life existential contact, (2) precocious existential awareness, and (3) a lack of support for the empathic sixth sense that is unique to the sensitivity and sensibility of OCD.

The first form of trauma—real-life existential contact—is the boundary experience of death itself, literally. We've seen this in examples of OCD sufferers who had early, real-life brushes with death such as a severe car accident, a death of a close relative, or some other early flooding of the emotional system with the specter of death.

We've also seen examples of the second form—those with OCD who have a precocious existential awareness of their and others' mortality from the very start. Without the emotional tools and relational guidance needed to productively ask and answer the tough questions that their awareness of mortality brought to mind, they instead spiraled into an infinite variety of obsessive-compulsive strategies to keep death at bay.

The third and final trauma that instigates OCD is a lack of support for and awareness of how difficult it is to carry a sixth sense of empathic sensitivity. Picking up on so much emotional material in their environments without the help of emotionally sensitive and intelligent relational partners leaves OCD sufferers at the mercy of their own minds to ground themselves. Unfortunately, because the mind can't really do this properly without the integration of feelings in the body, these OCD sufferers get totally out of alignment and overcompensate for their intense emotions with overactive, obsessional minds.

That said, when this capacity is identified, recognized, and nurtured, those who might otherwise develop OCD can instead develop the capacity to ask and answer the big questions of life creatively and find ample room to house the myriad and varied feelings they connect to so well. What can become an enormous downside and liability can easily be nurtured into a gift, strength, and power.

Trauma occurs when you can't maintain a coherent emotional story without serious shame, pain, humiliation, or fear. When this presses on the psyche, defenses come up to relieve you. Your highly expansive mind must manage these overwhelming feelings. This feeds the critic who saves you from psychic pain while sealing you off from creative living.

We see a most dramatic and artistic rendering of this seal-off in the recent short film *Waving* (Nyhus & Brumwell, 2022). The film begins with a man assiduously walking on the beach while keeping the world out with his black umbrella in the bright sun. A sign in the foreground reads: "Beware: Danger of being cut off by incoming tides."

The man proceeds to tell us that a kind woman once told him that his thoughts force him to be the center of the universe, holding it all together, as though his compulsions ensure the safety of everyone he loves. We are then taken into the cell of his mind, replete with messages from the critic: "You never loved them," "You are weak," "Sick coward," and "Do your duty." We hear the ringing in his ears of the critic's other choice statements: "You've abandoned your post," "Just fade away," and "You should have never been a father."

The critic keeps the man, named Charlie, away from the world, and distant from the important people in his life, who seem to call to him from an old ringing telephone and a television transmitting muffled and distorted voices. In an abandoned house on the beach that resembles a shipwreck, Charlie's family wonders where he is and if he can join them, but he appears paralyzed in his armchair.

Beginning to develop some distance from his critic, as if discovering his diagnosis for the first time, he writes the phrase "Our Cruel Demon." Soon after, a key emerges from his mouth, and he musters the power to close the television of his perpetual inner critic and open a door out of the abandoned house to the beach, where he returns to the inside of a large O-circle drawn in the sand.

At the conclusion of the film, Charlie watches, or possibly imagines, himself wading out into the water as if to drown, when a woman offers her assistance and brings him in from isolation. She reaches out, recognizing his exhaustion, and he simply tells her, "I need to contact my family."

This film illustrates how your critic flourishes when you retreat further and further inward, with little to no human warmth or love to accompany you. The statements voiced by Charlie's critic, likewise, are impersonal and cruel: "You've abandoned your post" and "Just fade away." And despite the best efforts of his family members, Charlie cannot speak out against his inner tormenters.

Waving (Nyhus & Brumwell, 2022) showcases the shame, isolation, confusion, and terror of being trapped inside one's own head. And to me, it also showcases the limits of treatments that merely focus on behavior and anxiety. Charlie is a good example of not only how terrifying undiagnosed OCD can be but how little is understood about how to work with the critic inside OCD through relationship.

In stark contrast, we have a scene from Steven Spielberg's film *The Fabelmans* (2022) that shows how the critic can be transformed into the muse *through* relationship. Spielberg, himself no stranger to anxiety, chronicles the story of his autobiographical alter-ego, Sammy Fabelman, as he navigates the conflicts between his head and heart, his mother and father, and his desire to serve his art and the potential to betray his own family.

What begins as confusing and irritating tension—the pressure from his father to put together a film compilation of a camping trip to console his mother who has just lost her own mother—transforms into a moment of awakening and an unexpected and unorthodox blessing from a circus man. Sammy's Uncle Boris, played to perfection by actor Judd Hirsch, is a lion tamer and film worker who is keenly aware of the heart-rending conflict between pursuing one's art and individuality, on the one hand, and honoring one's family and empathy, on the other. Or, as he says when Sammy contests the artistry of putting his head in a lion's mouth: "No. Sticking your head in the mouth of lions was balls! Making sure the lion don't eat my head??? That is art!!!" (Spielberg, 2022).

Boris tells Sammy, before he even realizes it himself, that he doesn't want to make the camping film because he really wants to finish the war film he's directing. He also clues him in to the hidden conflict between choosing family over art, and how it is already tormenting him. To illustrate, he grabs Sammy by the cheeks until it burns, and he recoils, proclaiming, like a benediction:

You will make your movies, and you will do your art, and you re-member how it hurt so you know what I'm saying: Art will give you crowns in heaven and laurels on earth. BUT!! It'll tear your heart out and leave you lonely. You'll be a shonde for your loved ones, an exile in the desert, a gypsy. Art is NO GAME!! Art is dangerous as a lion's mouth, it'll bite your head off!!

And yet, Spielberg, like Sammy, doesn't end up choosing between his own desire—to be an artist—and love and care for his family—his exquisite empathy. *The Fabelmans* both honors and laments the virtues and complications of his family and the ways it both shapes him and helps him find himself. Although Uncle Boris presents an either/or solution to his conflict, he gives Sammy the new creative possibility of having a both/and moment.

For many with OCD, these same either/or moments of choosing one's self-interest or one's empathy figure quite prominently. And just as Sammy needs a benevolent witness and spokesperson for his conflict, the brave kind who can literally put his head in the mouth of a lion, so too, those with OCD require support to be able to face and make something out of the profound ambivalence and conflict that arises from being so emotionally sensitive.

A ROUND-UP OF SKILLS TO TAME AND TRANSFORM THE CRITIC

The antidote to the critic comes in all the skills we've been working on. The critic within OCD will try to distract from key issues while trying to focus on them as well; the muse comes when we decode this and reconcile it. The critic has you dwell on one-dimensional, pure, and perfect negative instead of helping you explore, express, and contain nuance. The critic sells the fiction that you need to be totally good and right instead of allowing you to be temporarily bad, brash, and bold.

REVISITING VICIOUS CIRCLES

In its work of self-protection and defense, the critic ushers in a tragicomic feature: the irony of vicious circles. Psychologist Paul Wachtel (1993) writes brilliantly about the ways in which neurotic defenses operate in order to keep us away from our fears but then unwittingly cause those very fears to happen. We become victims when the difficult feelings that we temporarily ward off boomerang back at us with even more intensity, as is so often the case with OCD.

Wachtel (1993) gives the example, so apropos for those with OCD, of the individual afraid of his own anger. The more he attempts "to bury the anger and act unaggressive in the extreme" and suppresses his healthy aggressiveness and assertiveness, the more he becomes "frustrated, ignored, overshadowed, and treated as insignificant" (Wachtel, 1993, p. 22). He becomes angry, and yet, because he doesn't allow himself to be in touch with, or even aware of, his anger, it becomes all the more uncontrollable. He attempts to disguise or conceal his anger but it doesn't work and only begets more anger and greater defenses against that anger.

In John Green's novel *Turtles All the Way Down* (2017), protagonist Aza Holmes is haunted by the sudden death of her father and her OCD jumps in, both to protect her from and to persecute her for her overwhelming fear of life's fragility. Her OCD finds an ingenious way of expressing how delicate humans are by keying in on how easily bacteria, through the skin's microbiome, could take us over. Are we truly agents of a safe balance, or do our microbiomes really have the control? She notices how easy it is to get an infection and she obsesses about the possibility of C. diff—a germ that causes diarrhea and colitis—while repeatedly picking at and draining the puss from a never-fully-healed scab on her finger. The scab is a brilliant metaphor for the continually unhealed and ever-present wound of her father's death and her awareness of existential terror itself.

There is a surprising irony in Aza's behavior. Her attempts at illustrating her immense empathy and sensitivity regarding her father's loss, and the potential for loss of all of us in the human condition, leaves her perpetually lost and distracted by thought. In one pivotal scene, her best friend, Daisy Ramirez, calls her out on what she's missing, asking her if she even knows the name of her parents, their occupations, the name of her cat, and a litany of other personal details. Daisy bluntly makes the point that Aza's obsessional preoccupations make her quite self-centered despite her desired wish to be able to save herself and the world from bacterial annihilation.

Just as with the client with anger, Aza wants to do everything in her power to prevent harm and protect life and yet, ironically, she also shuts out the most important molecular details of her best friend's life because she is in thrall to the critic.

The central irony illustrated in both cases is that vital aspects of the self are cut off, relegated, denied, or minimized, as the critic gains power. And that critic has the ultimate end of protecting the self at an immense price: the loss of creative vitality, embodied connection, and mindful presence. The overly anxious need to be in control of the mind takes over and supplants the possibility for greater connection with the self and the world. This is the tragicomic outcome of the critic in full sway: an attempt to prevent a worst-case scenario from becoming an ironically and Kafkaesque new worst*est*-case scenario. Only, now, this has become institutionalized and familiarized as the only option.

Happily, there is a way out: through and even beyond the critic. Those with OCD can find their way through by revitalizing a creative and playful mode of engaging their feelings, thoughts, and circumstances. I recently saw a very wise and concise quote from an individual with OCD in recovery named Tia Wilson (2023). In it, she transforms the critic into the muse: "We are so good at 'solving away' our emotion. That's what my OCD journey has been all about. OCD is all about trying to escape the feelings through action, rather than just allowing them" (Wilson, 2023, para. 1).

Allowing this emotion and trying to make and find form in that feeling, even though it may seem difficult at first, is the way to transform vicious cycles into the virtuous circles of the muse.

THE MUSE FINDS FORM IN FEELING

Psychiatrist and therapist Roger Lewin (1997) illustrates the subtle beauty and power that OCD sufferers can use to find their way back to the muse. He chronicles the case of fifteen-year-old Felix, a patient who has just been released from a month-long hospital stay following a suicide attempt. Felix suffers from severe obsessions and compulsions; but as Dr. Lewin gets to know him better, he notices a special and hidden power that allows Felix to spontaneously play with both form and feeling. Safely protected from the critic—from its obsessions and compulsions that torment him daily with meaningless rituals and rumination—this hidden strength becomes the inspiration for both Felix's growth and the relationship he is developing with his therapist.

Felix shares his love for palindromes—words or phrases that read the same both forward and backward. And with great pride, he discloses one that he just created, which, not so surprisingly, expresses one of the major conflicts of his young life: "Ma is as selfless as I am."

Dr. Lewin is "stunned and delighted" at this "work of art" and further impressed by the sophistication and formal power of this atypical palindrome (Lewin, 1997 p. 10). In contrast to a simpler and more straightforward palindrome ("Able I was ere I saw Elba"), this one requires a frame shift in order to correctly read the phrase. Furthermore, it communicates volumes about the nature of his own personality, his mother's, and the relationship between them and the world. As Lewin notes: "this degree of flexibility in boundaries might be both a great asset and a great liability, vastly complicating and enriching the perceptual field, prejudicing in the direction of instability Felix showed me now only what he could do, but what he knew" (p. 10).

And even more importantly, like Tia Wilson (2023) advised above, it is crucial to stay with the feeling of what he is sharing: like his mother, Felix feels like he can give away too much. The feeling in this form is a useful, productive, and inspiring way for Felix and Dr. Lewin to create healthier boundaries and differentiation between him and his mother, and also a way for Dr. Lewin to help him to develop that in healthy competition as they discover new forms of understanding together.

One day, Felix decides that his first palindrome is quite clumsy and that he has found a more concise and clearer version. This was in effect a way to communicate that he had been working on sharpening himself and finding new forms that could be creative instead of, like his obsessions and compulsions, self-negating and repetitive. Dr. Lewin noted that it was a more open, empathetic, truthful, and much less despairing new version: "Ma is as I am."

It became the inspiration for the continued work of using the new relationship with Dr. Lewin to foster a sense of an independent voice in relation. As Dr. Lewin later notes to himself the uncanny coincidence—and perhaps his own playful use of form and feeling—that "Ma is" rendered backward produces "Siam," as in Siamese twins. Nothing can come closer to representing both the problem and possibility of having a twin in his mother and needing a new twin in his therapist with whom Felix can find a new balance of self in relationship to others.

Dr. Lewin notes something we've been tracking that forms the surprising upside of OCD: "I know that it sounds paradoxical and counterintuitive to say that, psychologically, we must often envision the solution before it is possible to have the problem" (Lewin, 1997, p. 12). Through his playful palindromes, Felix "saw clearly where his difficulties lay and what the way out was as a theoretical matter" (p. 12). One might even go further and suggest that it is no theoretical matter whatsoever: it is connecting life itself beyond his severe obsessions and compulsions. Throughout this book, in just about every case, I've been trying to show how within OCD's seeming problems solutions can also be found.

THE CRITIC AND THE MUSE TARGET
THE MOST PERSONAL SUFFERING

I've held off on sharing the most personal connection I've had to OCD until this chapter, and in many ways, to me, it makes the most sense here. The critic and muse within OCD always hits on the most personal and complex aspects of our stories. Like the story of Felix and his mother and Dr. Lewin, my family story also centers around finding a new way to balance the heightened sensitivity and pain of OCD.

My mother suffered throughout her life with washing and contamination OCD so much so that she was never without a bottle of rubbing alcohol and a host of tissues to open doors and wash our hands whenever we ventured out. It wasn't uncommon for the OCD to hit when we returned from some new or dirty place, like New York City of the 1980s and 1990s, or even just due to an emotional conflict not unlike those I've been describing thus far. Her OCD also found its way into minor checking rituals when we left the house for a trip: repeatedly making sure the door was locked and the stove was turned off.

But her OCD story starts way before the washing and checking that most people envision as classic OCD. My mother's parents were both immigrants from the Middle East—my grandmother was from Syria and my grandfather was from Israel. They made their way to Brooklyn via Panama, where my mother and her three siblings were born. My mother's parents divorced shortly after they made it to New York, and it was difficult for her mother to both practically and emotionally raise four children and be the main breadwinner. It was not uncommon for my mother, with her profound sensitivity, to both sense and companion her mother's pain and suffering. She became my grandmother's confidante, compensating for the chaos that occurred between my grandparents whenever they were together, and she played a stabilizing force of empathy amid the typical stresses of motherhood.

This blurry relationship unsurprisingly led to one of the first OCD symptoms my mother had: the fear that something might happen to her mother, and she would be alone and abandoned. It was a fear that I, too, would later experience as the son of a struggling single mother.

In my mother's and my own case, OCD was clearly a combination of nature and nurture. She had an innate sensitivity that enabled her to notice all the adversity around her, and she lacked the resources and support to make coherent and emotionally healthy sense of it all. Nor did she have the room or freedom to healthily oppose the circumstances or productively direct her anger and frustration; instead, her sensitivity became the emotional stitches tenuously holding a wounded family together.

The muse that eventually turned into the OCD critic started out in my mother's case as follows. Because my grandmother and the general culture failed to recognize, identify, and mitigate my mother's precocious sensitivity, it became a problem. It was the thing that she often felt ashamed about. Why couldn't she be more independent and stronger? Why did she wrestle with such a continual fear of death and chaos? She never felt entitled to have healthy boundaries, because, if she did, she'd break down the very system that was meant to hold her up.

My mother's compulsions to wash her hands were frequently triggered after being recruited into carrying too much of other's emotional mess. With no relationship to help verbalize her profound empathy and disgust for being placed in such an impossible role, her critic took over.

Later, when she later met and married my father, my mother saw promise and hope in his strength. As a refugee from Egypt who had brought his own family to America and earned his way through higher education and a successful career, my father seemed to have everything my mother felt was missing in herself. He was not overloaded by emotional sensitivity and was extraordinarily self-sufficient and confident. In attempting to find the underdeveloped side of herself, she married him, half hoping that she would gain her undeveloped sides and he would discover his.

Unfortunately, what occurred instead was a repetition of the OCD critic, her sensitivity again being considered "too much," problematic, and disruptive. My father's response to her emotional challenges was to try to push her to be more alpha like he was, and yet it only separated her from herself and made her feel even more like a failure.

The alpha or the omega didn't work for my parents in resolving my mother's OCD, nor does it work in the treatments that I've seen in the OCD field. Either/or solutions aren't the answer. Just as Kafka was writing from a place of personal suffering, he also had something extremely important to shine light on with respect to the culture. My hope is that the way I'm bringing these aspects together—from a very personal place too—shines a light on an important facet needed for better OCD treatment in our culture today.

THE FINE LINE BETWEEN OBSESSION AND CREATIVITY

Dacher Keltner (2009) writes that "survival of the kindest," rather than survival of the fittest, would have been a better catchphrase for Charles Darwin. Not only did he feel "the world's pain so acutely, and so persistently," as one biographer writes (Valiunas, 2009), but Darwin also viewed extending one's heart in compassion to others as "one of the noblest" moral achievements (Cain, 2022). Moved upon hearing this parallel to the Buddha's teachings, the Dalai Lama declared: "I will now call myself a Darwinian" (Ekman, 2010; Cain, 2022)."

Darwin used his generous heart—affected in his youth by the stinging death of his mother, and later in adulthood by the untimely passing of his beloved ten-year-old daughter—to search for what keeps the course of natural history ticking. Illustrating the depth of his sensitivity, Cain (2022) writes that Darwin:

> noted example after example of beings reacting to the suffering of other beings: The dog who takes care, every time he passed it, to lick a sick cat in his household. The crows who patiently fed their blind and elderly companion. The monkey who risked his life to save a beloved zookeeper from a hostile baboon.

There's something instructive about how Charles Darwin lived with his own nagging OCD critic—perpetual worries about his and his children's health and well-being, concerns about being misunderstood and hurting others, and fears about whether he had worked hard enough—and used the upside of OCD—a generous heart and expansive mind—in service of innovative and revolutionary scientific advances and personal growth as well. Darwin biographer Janet Browne notes that although the tender care of his older sisters and the strong relationship with his older brother and father eased the blow, Darwin remained haunted by the suddenness of his mother's death. As she writes: "Perhaps only his great pleasure in natural history, which in later days verged on the obsessive, can be seen as a first step in a general retreat from the frightening intensity of emotions in the real world" (Browne, 2010, p. 22).

Or, as we discussed in the previous chapter, perhaps it was Darwin's early awareness of the disconcerting existential realities of the world that led him to pursue and develop mastery over them through his studies about how life continually goes on. Either way, it is clear that Darwin's obsessional tendencies found creative purpose, form, and possibility in the pursuit of new discovery. We can speculate that this became a way to integrate what he felt in the natural habitat of his early childhood with the newly possible within the exciting and ever-expanding world of science and exploration. It is as if the upside of OCD had informed him to keep on pursuing the leads that would bring him to his great revelations about the triumph of life over death.

Browne (2010) writes: "His growing dependence on natural history may well have begun as a defence mechanism bringing some sort of consolation in its wake" (p. 27). And yet, I suspect that science was more than just a container for his grief; it, alongside the loving support of his family, enabled him to develop his scientific theories in parallel to his own person. Connecting to the *Something Else* (to borrow writer Sarah Wilson's felicitous phrase), Darwin learned to directly tap into the source of the muse.

FROM HYPERVIGILANCE TO MINDFUL CREATIVITY

The critic that controls and governs OCD is hypervigilant. This should come as no surprise given its function as a survival mechanism to protect from retraumatization. Vigilance arises when we are in a state of true danger and threat.

Harvard psychologist and researcher Ellen Langer (1997) notes that attention is a very dynamic, fluid, and contextual capacity, and yet, many of us, even in nontraumatic situations, attempt to keep that attention fixed and solid. From our earliest experiences in school and even at home with our families, we are quickly socialized and criticized about not being able to "just keep still and pay attention." But of course, attention doesn't work like this.

Langer (1997) notes that it is not only impossible to keep our attention so fixed, but it is extremely fatiguing as well. She gives the example of how overly vigilant she became as a new horseback rider, constantly on the lookout for overhanging branches. When she allowed herself to practice more "soft vigilance," not only did she better notice the branches and enjoy the ride more, but she was also better prepared for other potential obstacles and dangers on the trail.

Both the obsessions and compulsions in OCD proceed along the narrow lines of this fixed attention and hypervigilance. All you can think about is the thing you shouldn't be doing and why it's totally bad and wrong; you focus on what will immediately get rid of the anxiety and make it better. This hypervigilance is ruled by the critic who does not allow you to see anything beyond the blinders it has placed on you.

As we talked about in earlier chapters, the critic doesn't let you have fuller contact with your selves, with all the emotions of your current situation (the anger as well as the fear, the hatred as well as the love, etc.), with the possible nuance existing within what at first appears to be only negative.

But there is another option. This option is on the side of what Langer (1997) calls "soft vigilance," which allows you to take in a greater variety of information about your thoughts and feelings and a fuller context of why they are occurring. All along, I've been showcasing this option by decoding the message that OCD is trying to tell you, by exploring how it's trying to add more complexity and nuance to the emotional picture, and by demonstrating how you can use its upside magic to become stronger in yourself and your relationships.

Soft vigilance naturally leads to what Langer has been writing and researching about for years, noting its myriad benefits on self-efficacy, agency, happiness, productivity, and peace of mind. She has researched its benefits in a variety of populations and situations. And it all fits under the simple yet profound phrase "mindful creativity."

Mindful creativity is the capacity to notice and make novel distinctions out of whatever you are experiencing and, in so doing, to become more psychologically creative with it (Langer, 1997). As an example, in one study, Langer and her colleagues taught people undergoing major surgery to look at other angles of their hospital experience, to notice some hidden advantages such as having more time to be in touch with family and to reexamine their life goals, or even their forced weight loss. Patients in this mindful group showed lower stress levels, took fewer pain medications, and left the hospital sooner than those in the nonmindful condition (Langer, 1997).

OCD is quick to have the critic zone you into your fear and perceptions of badness or wrongness without ever allowing you to explore what might be right, interesting, or worthwhile about the feelings and thoughts you're experiencing. It also tends to overvalue negative thoughts and feelings as if they are static and permanent rather than momentary and partial explorations of a fuller context at play.

Through his use of palindromes, Felix playfully explores new dimensions of his relationship with his mother and himself. Darwin, too, was able to convert much of his hypervigilance into a mindful creativity about what he explored and examined in the natural world.

When Aza Holmes tells her psychiatrist, Dr. Singh, that she isn't driving the bus of her own consciousness, that she's crazy, and that there's hardly any possible way to be a singular self if she is acknowledging sides of herself, such as her own cruelty, Dr. Singh replies with mindful creativity: "Self is a plurality, but pluralities can also be integrated, right? Think of a rainbow. It's one arc of light, but also seven differently colored arcs of light" (Green, 2017, p. 87).

Aza can't see herself other than being out of control, the same bacteria that keeps us alive can only be her undoing. She should be able to have a self that somehow transcends this universally human/ bacterial symbiosis. All Aza can be in touch with is the fear of death, the loss of agency, and the heartbreaking irreconcilability that we will (and do) lose the people we love the most, including ourselves. How loving and selfless is this, and yet so self-interested and selfish?

Yes, this is what being human is, but Aza's OCD doesn't let her delve into this messy and difficult emotional territory and instead uses her sanitized mind to keep it all in check. As she says to the boyfriend she keeps pushing away, "It made no sense. I was a story riddled with plot holes" (Green, 2017, p. 253). Of course, keeping this in check in her mind and not examining the plot holes with her heart is the ironic way that OCD makes her lose control.

MINDSIGHT TO THE RESCUE

All of the skills I've been outlining fall under the concept of "mindsight" developed by noted psychiatrist and author Daniel J. Siegel (2010). Like mindful creativity, mindsight is the capacity to be simultaneously receptive and discriminating. It enables us to carefully attend to the inner workings of our minds without being "swept away" by the challenging and difficult currents within. It also supports us in moving beyond repetitive emotional loops and the "autopilot of ingrained behaviors" (Siegel, 2010, p. ix). By tapping into what is not fully conscious, we begin to "name and tame" overwhelming emotions, and in so doing, develop greater clarity, specificity, and nuance in our experience for ourselves and our relationships.

Siegel refers to this capacity to look within and reflect on our experience as our seventh sense. His take on mindsight is perfectly tailored to the ongoing dilemmas and challenges of those who struggle with OCD. It answers the questions at the heart of OCD: "How can we be receptive to the mind's riches and not just reactive to its reflexes? How can we direct our thoughts and feelings rather than be driven by them?" (p. xi). And it is the foundation for turning the critic I've been describing, here and throughout this book, into the muse of well-being and integration.

I've shown how OCD can do so much more than just tear you apart. When you are able to work all the different angles of OCD— the range and depth of feeling it presents, the expansive and imaginative thoughts it generates—and carry these with a healthy dose of pride and humility, you have found your way to the upside.

This is *the muse*, the virtuous circle, the mindsight that helps painter Cristi López both experience and express the fullness of her story in life and in art, author John Green to explore the challenges and beauties of being alive in a world that seems on the precipice of death, musician Joe Alterman find new licks on the piano to set new standards and rewrite the repetitive story of his life with OCD, Greta Thunberg to find the courage to call the world to attention and fight climate change, and Charles Darwin to keep searching for our unexpected origins among the apes.

THE MUSE FLOURISHES IN A BOTH/AND APPROACH TO LIFE

The muse within your OCD critic emerges when you take a both/and approach to living. It materializes when your thoughts are embodied and felt in a real, tangible, and humanly imperfect way, and when your feelings can be mindfully mined and sharpened into diamonds of myriad facets. The muse is the blending of the imaginary and the real, where the literal and the figurative coexist and play off of each other to create more than either can alone. It is the coexistence of the polarities of good and bad, the right and wrong, and the pure and profane. It is also the simultaneous awareness of stability and variety, what feels in control and what feels out of control. And most importantly, it is the unique integration of what is ultimately known (this life) and what is ultimately unknown and mysterious (death and a possible afterlife). All of these either/or uncertainties transform themselves into both/ and possibilities, and in so doing, they create the necessary tension required for a creative, fulfilling, and integrated life.

As Aza Holmes puts it most poetically at the close of *Turtles All the Way Down*, echoing Robert Frost's summary of everything he learned about life: "I, a singular proper noun, would go on, if always in a conditional tense" (Green, 2017, p. 285).

EXERCISE: FREEWRITE YOUR WAY PAST THE CRITIC

It's not easy getting past the critic, but there's nothing like an improvisational approach to make it happen and free up the muse. Similar to Julia Cameron's method in *The Artist's Way* (1992), this exercise asks you to write about everything that the critic is trying to throw your way and to put it out on the table so you can really inspect it and make the connections you need to have a true conversation rather than an interrogation.

Your mission is to freewrite (with as little self-censoring as possible) whatever you are thinking and feeling when your critic strikes and encourage yourself to openly explore the fuller context of your story. Don't worry about grammar or punctuation, and trust that this process will open new possibilities if you allow your other sides to show up.

The critic has a way of silencing and sidelining other sides of the self, and so your goal here is to invite these sides to the table to get more airtime and join in the conversation. The critic is trying to protect you, but it is also trying to imprison the more spontaneous sides that you need to truly figure out the issues with which you are struggling.

Allow your inner child, your trickster, and your rebel to come up in the new things you are seeing and hearing as you look at whatever is bringing on your critic right now. And just write without worrying, stopping, or censoring.

What is the critic trying to scare you with? Does it have any unexpected or hidden reasons it's trying to help you, things that might actually be considered "good"? Are there any other sides of yourself that it isn't allowing to have a voice? What might those sides truly wish to say?

Notice your inner critic trying to inhibit and deter you, even as you try this exercise. It might be telling you that this is silly and a waste of your time. Or it might by asking you why you don't you already have this figured and insisting that you should be in better control of yourself.

Write whatever the critic is saying to you and notice how it attempts to sow doubt, confusion, and fear in you like Iago does to Othello. Type or handwrite it out: "I don't really know why I'm feeling so anxious, and this writing is just so stupid, who am I to think that I can get beyond this without following the obsession or compulsion of my critic?"

Personify the critic. Does it remind you of an internet troll, a drill sergeant, a football coach, or a stage mom? Does it remind you of any prior critics in your past? Family members? Teachers? Classmates? See if you can write about them and how they had—or still have—a hold on you.

Notice the critic's savagery as one observes one's does "monkey mind" attacking during meditation. Is the critic trying to insult, demean, or attack you? Proclaim, "I see you, critic, and I choose to come back to my breath and my freewriting."

Are there understandable and sensible reasons your critic needed to protect you from shame, humiliation, or pain? If so, give it credit, and kindly ask for the fuller story, so you can help the critic begin to work with the muse.

FEED THE MUSE, STARVE THE CRITIC

Julia Cameron (1992) swears by the two strategies of freewriting that she calls (1) "the morning pages" and (2) "the artist date." We will adapt the second strategy here for the purpose of feeding the muse.

Is it possible for you to take a break from the critic's bombardment and engage in something creative and artistic? It could be music, photography, painting, books, movies, sports, or anything else that allows you to move into a flow state.

Is it possible for you to be replenished in a way that helps you put artistic form to what initially seemed like nothing more than a critical and destructive OCD spiral? Notice how painter Cristi López didn't shy away from her critic and its fears, incorporating the feared scissors (a great symbol of the critic) into the fuller vision of her art. Notice how author John Green (2017) found an artful way to describe the thought spirals of his character Aza and also express a part of himself. Your mission here is to use art, both outside of you and inside of yourself, to feed your muse and starve your critic.

8

BECOMING YOURSELF
WITH AND BEYOND OCD

In his novel *Bewilderment*, Richard Powers sums up the spirit and purpose of my hopeful and subversive take on OCD best: "Life is something we need to stop correcting. My boy was a pocket universe I could never hope to fathom. Every one of us is an experiment, and we don't even know what the experiment is testing. . . . *Nobody's perfect. . . . But, man, we all fall short so beautifully*" (Power, 2021, p. 5, emphasis in original).

I don't want you to come away from this book overthinking your OCD or, worse yet, overidentifying as someone with OCD. OCD is about something much bigger and more beautiful than a diagnosis. It's about having a heart and mind that's tuned in to the never-ending changes of being human, a tune that goes on and on, always seeking new harmonies. OCD scares you because it recognizes life's hidden poetry; it recognizes that while love outlasts time, we must lose ourselves and each other too.

How is it possible to both care and not care about this heartbreaking gift that OCD reminds you of daily? How is it possible to remember that your center will hold while everything constantly changes? Such is the miraculous task set before you as an individual with OCD.

With that exquisitely sensitive heart and roving imaginative mind, you've been left on your own to make sense of it all. And at times, it's just been too much. But it doesn't have to be like that anymore. This book is your new map.

My paradoxical take on OCD is captured beautifully by Carl Jung: "It seems that all true things must change and only that which changes remains true" (quoted in Stulberg, 2023, p. 74). This is the embodiment and essence of OCD's upside. The upside comes in being able to transform the negative into nuance, to hold space for the multiplicity and complexity within, and to engage more interdependently and collaboratively with others from your solid center. Instead of trying to control all of the changes you are able to perceive due to your emotional sensitivity, you make something beautiful out of them.

Best-selling author, researcher, and coach Brad Stulberg (2023) writes eloquently about how to tap into the creativity found within the heart of change. It's built into our very biology. You might have been taught that homeostasis—the return to a former equilibrium—is the overarching rule of life, but it's the capacity to continually develop a new order, known as allostasis, which truly drives us. Instead of being tethered to a stable, set point, allostasis enables us to find a balance that incorporates the old and the new, honoring the dynamic, ever-changing possibilities of ourselves and the world. This capacity to remain the same while changing is the hallmark of creative living.

MOVING FROM EITHER/OR TO BOTH/AND

OCD interrogates you with the bigger questions of existence without learning to trust in the essential flow of creative life. It's what finally leads Aza, at the conclusion of *Turtles All the Way Down* (Green, 2017), to find her own perspective in this vast universe.

Sitting under the night sky with her first love whom she will momentarily lose, looking at Polaris and reflecting on light now seen from 425 years ago, she recognizes a heretofore unseen truth. There is something magical about being with your vastness and your smallness simultaneously. She speaks directly to her OCD thought spirals in one planetary-sized epiphany:

> Spirals grow infinitely small the farther you follow them inward, but they also grow infinitely large the farther you follow them out. And I knew I would remember that feeling . . . back before the machinery of fate ground us into one thing or another, back when we could still be everything. (Green, 2017, p. 284)

The only way through OCD, as Aza shows us, is through relationship, the prism through which all of the impersonal forces of the mind and the universe are humanized and that allows us to keep everything in proper scope.

BUT WHO AM I WITHOUT OCD? WAIT, DON'T GO!

There's no doubt that many of you out there, dear readers, will want to cling to your OCD label because it is still very much a part of you—that wild thing we've made beautiful. As OCD advocate and author Allison Raskin writes:

> I have always been someone who is averse to calling my OCD a superpower. It has caused me too much harm over the years for me to think of it fondly in any way. But when I begin to think about myself without it, I start to panic. And this bothers me. How can I want to keep something that has kept me prisoner since I was four years old? Why don't I trust that Allison alone is good enough to flourish and remain clean? How warped must my sense of self be? At this point in my journey, I don't have the answers to those questions. But I am glad I am starting to ask them. (Raskin, 2023a, para. 7)

Raskin isn't alone in just starting to ask these questions. As a culture and as a field, we are only now beginning to recognize the full depth, complexity, and beauty of this beast that is OCD, and we are still mostly ambivalent and unsure about how we can reconcile such challenging implications.

The ambitious goal of this book has been to challenge the conventional understandings of OCD and meet fire with fire. It's here to question all the false either/or conceptions of OCD. Either you accept that your OCD has no meaning, or you suffer! Either you deal with your OCD behaviors in an alpha way by confronting the bully with exposure exercises, or you're an omega failure who's not doing it right! Either your OCD is just in your nature, in the quirky wiring and misfiring of your brain, or you've been blaming yourself all along for overestimating the dangers in your environment. Silly, human, it could never be both your nature and nurture.

The both/and approach that I'm forwarding isn't meant to upset the applecart, it's meant to widely embrace the full humanity of your OCD. On a personal note, writing about OCD has been to interrogate my own experience more fully and to give back life to the one who gave me life too. My hope is that it brings life back to you as well.

FROM MINDLESS REPETITION TO MINDFUL CREATIVITY

I was working on the proof of one of my poems all the morning and took out a comma. In the afternoon I put it back again.

—OSCAR WILDE (OFTEN ATTRIBUTED)

Echoing the Oscar Wilde quote above, Penelope, in Homer's *The Odyssey*, showcases the inner ambivalence and conflict that guides the OCD mind. While waiting nearly twenty years for her husband Odysseus's safe return from the Trojan War, in order to hold off the one-hundred-plus suitors vying for her hand in marriage, Penelope weaves a burial shroud on her loom during the day and unravels all of her work by night. Relational psychoanalyst Stephen Mitchell (1988) first uses this wonderful analogy to describe the way that all individuals struggling with neurotic conditions unwittingly undo their own progress.

OCD works like this mindless repetition too, promising to solve all of your problems if you do its bidding and then undoing all of your feelings of security, freedom, and control. As I've shown throughout this book, it has a unique sleight of hand that can only be discerned with practice. OCD takes you into thought spirals and exhausts you with repetitive fears, but you can also find your way back to mindful creativity. How can you do this? Let's recap how we've found our way to the upside of OCD.

We began by identifying and noticing your keen, empathic sensitivity and relying on the information it shares to get closer to the *heart* of your OCD rather than getting lost in its *thoughts*. This step helped you rediscover a foundational part of your temperament and nature— one that just needs to be acknowledged rather than fixed. Best of all, this sensibility isn't pathological but, rather, is a capacity that needs support to be adequately tempered and tuned, just as a piano must by maintained by the sensitive ear and tools of the piano master.

Next, we noticed the quickness with which your imagination runs wild and sensitizes you toward the negative as a way of attempting to oversimplify the richness of your thought and feeling. Without easy categories to contain and express the nuance that you actually experience, your OCD mind takes over and tries to manage your world by conjuring every possible negative scenario imaginable.

After moving beyond your feelings (your heart) and your thoughts (your mind), we moved into how OCD functions in your relationships. OCD does your dirty work by helping you to maintain and build healthier interpersonal boundaries. The quickness with which you are able to empathize and merge with the experience of others makes you more easily susceptible to losing yourself, and OCD is a surprising way of alerting you to this blurriness. We began to examine OCD as a friend and messenger instead of as just an enemy.

Without this important relational awareness, it is easy for others to unknowingly colonize your headspace and heartspace. This gets converted into the kinds of troubling obsessions and compulsions that seek to clear and clean up space for your own thoughts, feelings, and self-interest. Unfortunately, without making this link, the valuable message gets lost. Instead, it gets distorted and implemented in a self-defeating and literal fashion.

We noticed how OCD attempts to suppress your wild, trickster side in favor of the more traditionally good, moral, and righteous sides. We tracked how these wild sides are necessary for living with the kind of complexity and contradiction that you allow for others but not yourself.

Most importantly, we drilled down to the core of OCD: a profound and precocious existential awareness that sensitizes you not only to loss but also to the fragile beauty of life itself. We explored how being in touch with these questions in a creative way with proper support could make it possible to make this experience creative and awe-inspiring rather than terrifying.

Finally, we showed how to temper the critic that directs the OCD system of doubt, fear, and uncertainty, and return home to an ever-present state of mindful creativity. It's been a journey through the labyrinth of OCD, and yet, happily, together we've found a thread that helps us find our way through.

WHY THIS NEW INNER STORY MATTERS TO THE WORLD

Aside from illuminating the more nuanced inner story of OCD, the most poignant and practical purpose of writing this book is to address a significant problem that hardly gets airtime. A 2023 study (Kochar et al., 2023) found that the economic fallout of unsuccessfully treating OCD is a staggering 5 billion dollars per year in the United Kingdom alone. This enormous figure consists of 378 million dollars in therapy services and the remaining 4.7 billion dollars largely accrued from work absence. What I find even more heartbreaking is that a condition with such an outsized effect on society's productivity and well-being has had such limited treatment options with which to heal it.

In our culture today, there is a virtual monopoly on what is considered "proper" OCD treatment. It is either exposure and response prevention (ERP), acceptance-commitment therapy (ACT), or medication, and that's it. My hope in writing this book is that we will dig a lot deeper to find new and more integrated ways of helping and healing OCD for the sake of individuals and the culture at large. We've seen the examples of many luminaries struggling with OCD who have still been able to bring innovation and creativity to the world. What if there are many more out there who can contribute to business, science, the arts, and everything else under the sun with their expansive minds and generous hearts?

According to a recent study, Ziegler et al. (2021), it takes an average of seventeen years for someone with OCD to receive adequate therapy. Many claim that this shocking number is a result of the shame and stigma experienced by those suffering in silence, the lack of training in specialized OCD treatment, and/or the capacity of those with OCD to hide their symptoms and pass as unaffected. But I wonder if a significant reason why more people with OCD don't find or receive adequate care is because current treatments don't speak to their lived experience.

Does the treatment out there really appreciate, understand, and explain the overly generous and empathic heart of those with OCD? Does it see the creative possibility and power within the expansive mind and creative prowess of the OCD sufferer? Does it pay heed to the inner story and potential trauma that can originate or even exacerbate OCD?

Sadly, I fear that, as a field and culture, we have moved to either/or decisions regarding OCD—moving from an emotional and relational early theory to a biobehavioral one—that has thrown the baby out with the bathwater. *For more people to be helped in less time, more*

compassionately and comprehensively, we must incorporate a both/and ap-
proach to OCD, one that unites nature with nurture, the heart with the mind,
and the problem with the possibility.

My hope is that this is only the beginning of reconciling and integrating how OCD is brought on biologically and how it heals or degenerates based on one's environment. The both/and approach to OCD allows us to unite and reconcile these two spheres while also offering new possibilities for how individuals with OCD can work with it to the benefit of themselves and society. As surely as the common frame of reference has posited OCD as merely a deficit, problem, or even a madness, there is a vast, hidden world waiting to be discovered if we are willing to stay a while, to make room for it to unravel, to take time to decipher its code, and to endeavor to express its hidden nuances. This is the upside that we've been searching for throughout these pages, and this is where the beginning of becoming most fully you—OCD included—takes flight.

BIBLIOGRAPHY

Abramowitz, J. (2018, September). The inhibitory learning approach to exposure and response prevention. *The OCD newsletter.* https://iocdf .org/expert-opinions/the-inhibitory-learning-approach-to-exposure -and-response-prevention/.

Alcée, M. D. (2005). Revitalizing a relational view of obsessive-compulsive disorder: Explicit and implicit measurement of the working models of OCD subjects. Unpublished Dissertation, Fordham University.

———. (2020, January 19). OCD is a fire to be harnessed: A new way to understand a troubling disorder. *Psychology Today* [Blog]. https://www .psychologytoday.com/us/blog/live-life-creatively/202001/ocd-is -fire-be-harnessed.

———. (2020, February 10). Finding your way out of OCD: Tips for not missing your local train. *Psychology Today* [Blog]. https://www .psychologytoday.com/us/blog/live-life-creatively/202002/finding-your -way-out-ocd.

———. (2021, June 30). OCD from the inside-out: New thoughts on an old tormentor. *Psychology Today* [Blog]. https://www.psychologytoday.com /us/blog/live-life-creatively/201906/ocd-the-inside-out.

———. (2021, September 20). Find your feelings, not your anxiety: A kinder, gentler exposure-response prevention for OCD. *Psychology Today* [Blog]. https://www.psychologytoday.com/us/blog/live-life-crea tively/202109/find-your-feelings-not-your-anxiety.

———. (2022, March 22). The art of changing while staying the same for people with OCD: Do you struggle with the ups and downs of OCD? *Psychology Today* [Blog]. https://www.psychologytoday .com/us/blog/live-life-creatively/202203/the-art-changing-while -staying-the-same-people-ocd.

———. (2022, November 29). Why OCD treatment can fail: "Six degrees of Kevin Bacon" to the rescue. *Psychology Today* [Blog]. https://

www.psychologytoday.com/us/blog/live-life-creatively/202211
/why-ocd-treatment-can-fail.

———. (2022, December 24). OCD as a superpower: Here's how to harness
it and heal yourself. *Psychology Today* [Blog]. https://www.psychology
today.com/us/blog/live-life-creatively/202212/ocd-as-a-superpower.

———. (2022). *Therapeutic improvisation: How to stop winging it and own it as a
therapist.* W.W. Norton & Company.

———. (2023, February 5). Flip the script on OCD: A new CBT approach that moves from Kafka to Keats. *Psychology Today* [Blog]. https://
www.psychologytoday.com/us/blog/live-life-creatively/202302
/flip-the-script-on-ocd.

———. (2023, April 3). Who's trivializing OCD? A personal perspective:
Reclaiming the narrative of a misunderstood diagnosis. *Psychology Today*
[Blog]. https://www.psychologytoday.com/us/blog/live-life-creatively
/202304/whos-trivializing-ocd.

———. (2023, April 4). There's more to OCD than you think: A conversation with Cristi López. *Psychology Today* [Blog]. https://www
.psychologytoday.com/us/blog/live-life-creatively/202303/theres-more
-to-ocd-than-you-think-a-conversation-with-cristi-lopez.

———. (2023, May 23). Why focusing on feelings can help heal OCD: Your
feelings just might save you from all that anxiety. *Psychology Today*
[Blog]. https://www.psychologytoday.com/us/blog/live-life-creatively
/202305/why-focusing-on-feelings-can-help-heal-ocd.

———. (2023, May 31). Why the anxiety? Befriend your OCD and get
back to yourself. *Psychology Today* [Blog]. https://www.psychology
today.com/us/blog/live-life-creatively/202305/why-the-anxiety
-befriend-your-ocd-and-get-back-to-yourself.

———. (2023, October 8). Shouldn't we treat the heart of OCD too?
A personal perspective: Increasing treatment options for OCD.
Psychology Today [Blog]. https://www.psychologytoday.com/us/blog
/live-life-creatively/202310/shouldnt-we-treat-the-heart-of-ocd-too.

———. (2023, November 2). The generous heart and creative mind
within OCD: Let's rethink and reimagine CBT treatment for OCD.
Psychology Today [Blog]. https://www.psychologytoday.com/us/blog
/live-life-creatively/202311/the-generous-heart-and-creative-mind
-within-ocd-0.

———. (2023, November 11). Tapping the hidden potential inside OCD:
A personal perspective: I found parallels in Adam Grant's new book.

Psychology Today [Blog]. https://www.psychologytoday.com/us/blog/live-life-creatively/202310/tapping-the-hidden-potential-inside-ocd.

———. (2023, December 6). Don't be the grinch: Unwrapping OCD's greatest fear for the holidays. *Psychology Today* [Blog]. https://www.psychology today.com/us/blog/live-life-creatively/202312/dont-be-the-grinch.

———. (2023, December 15). Why ERP may not be enough for some OCD sufferers: Breaking the taboo of talk therapy. *Psychology Today* [Blog]. https://www.psychologytoday.com/us/blog/live-life-creatively/20 2312/why-erp-may-not-be-enough-for-some-ocd-sufferers.

Alcée, M. D., & Sager, T. A. (2017). How to fall in love with time-limited therapy: Lessons from poetry and music. *Journal of College Student Psychotherapy*, *31*(3), 203–214. doi:10.1080/87568225.2016.1276420.

Alterman, J. (2016, February 11). How music helped my struggles with OCD. *Riley's Wish Foundation* [Blog]. https://www.rileyswish.com/blog/2016/2/11/how-music-helped-my-struggles-wocd-by-joe-alterman.

Appelo, T. (2019, August 6). Toni Morrison: "National treasure." AARP. Retrieved March 8, 2024, from https://www.aarp.org/entertainment/books/info-2019/toni-morrison-national-treasure.html.

Aron, E. N. (1996). *The highly sensitive person*. Broadway.

Atlas, G. (2023). *Emotional inheritance: A therapist, her patients, and the legacy of trauma*. Little, Brown Spark.

Barrie, J. M. (2022). *Peter Pan* (F. D. Bedford, Illus.). Reader's Library Classics.

Batchelor, S. (2019, September 24). When to let go of the Dharma, too: A secular Buddhist teacher considers the parable of the raft and how once helpful things can become a burden instead. *Tricycle*. https://tricycle.org/article/buddhist-parable-of-the-raft/.

Bearman, M. (2023, May 11). Obsessive compulsive disorder with Joe Alterman [Audio podcast episode]. *Mind of a Song* [Podcast]. https://megbearmancounseling.com/blog/obsessive-compulsive-disorder-with-joe-alterman/.

Begley, S. (2018). *Can't. Just. Stop.: An investigation of compulsions*. Simon & Schuster Paperbacks.

Brady, D. (2019, April 2). Greta Thunberg and the enigma of disability. LinkedIn https://www.linkedin.com/pulse/greta-thunberg-enigma-dis ability-diane-brady/.

Brock, H., & Hany, M. (2023, May 29). *Obsessive compulsive disorder*. National Library of Medicine. https://www.ncbi.nlm.nih.gov/books/NBK553162/.

Bromberg, P. M. (2013). *Awakening the dreamer clinical journeys*. Taylor and Francis.

Browne, J. (2010). *Charles Darwin: A biography*, vol. 1, *Voyaging*. Vintage Digital.

Cain, S. (2013). *Quiet: The power of introverts in a world that can't stop talking*. Broadway Paperbacks.

Cain, S. (2023). Bittersweet: How sorrow and longing make us whole. Penguin Books.

Cameron, J. (1992). *The artist's way: A spiritual path to higher creativity*. Jeremy P. Tarcher/Perigee.

Cohen, L. (1988, May 9). How the heart approaches what it yearns: Interview with Leonard Cohen presented by John McKenna. Leonardcohenfiles .com. Retrieved February 27, 2024, from https://www.leonardcohen files.com/rte.html.

———. (1992). Anthem [Recorded by Leonard Cohen] *On the Future* [LP] Columbia.

———. (2000). Good advice for someone like me. Leonard Cohen Files. https://www.leonardcohenfiles.com/goodadvice.html.

Coogan, M., Brettler, M., Newsom, C., & Perkins, P. (2018). *The new Oxford annotated Bible with apocrypha: New revised standard version* (5th ed.). Oxford University Press.

Dahl, R. (2013). *Matilda*. Puffin.

David, L., & Seinfeld, J. (Program creators). (1989–1998). Seinfeld [Television show]. West-Shapiro & Castle Rock Entertainment.

David, S. (2018). *Emotional agility*. Penguin USA.

de Botton, A. (2016, May 28). Why you will marry the wrong person. *New York Times*. Retrieved from: https://www.nytimes.com/2016/05/29 /opinion/sunday/why-you-will-marry-the-wrong-person.html.

de Saint-Exupery, A. (1971). *The little prince* (K. Woods, Trans.). Harvest.

Dickinson, E. (2016). *The collected poems of Emily Dickinson*. First Avenue Editions.

Dostoevsky, F. (1993). *Crime and punishment* (R. Pevear & L. Volokhonsky, Trans.). Vintage Classics.

Dunn, S. (2000). *Different hours*. Norton.

Dusick, R. (2022). *Harder to breathe: A memoir of making Maroon 5, losing it all, and finding recovery*. BenBella Books.

Ekman, P. (2009, June). The Dalai Lama is a Darwinian. *Greater Good Magazine*. https://greatergood.berkeley.edu/video/item/the_dalai_lama _is_a_darwinian.

Farmer, S. (2019, December 12). How Greta Thunberg's autism helped make her the world's most important person for 2020. *The Hill*. https://thehill .com/changing-america/well-being/468091-opinion-activist.

Felisati, D., & Sperati, G. (2005, October 25). Franz Kafka. National Library of Medicine. https://www.ncbi.nlm.nih.gov/pmc/articles/PMC 2639911/.

Fichter, M. M. (1988). Franz Kafkas Magersucht [Franz Kafka's anorexia nervosa]. *Fortschritte der Neurologie-Psychiatrie, 56*(7), 231–238. DOI: 10.1055/s-2007-1001787.

Flood, A. (2017, October 14). John Green: "Having OCD is an ongoing part of my life." *The Guardian*. https://www.theguardian.com/books/2017 /oct/14/john-green-turtles-all-the-way-down-ocd-interview.

Freud, S. (1963). *Three case histories: The "wolf man," "the rat man," and the psychotic Doctor Schreber*. Collier Books.

Freud, S., & Gay, P. (1995). *The Freud reader*. Vintage.

Frost, R. (1931, February). Education by poetry. Retrieved February 27, 2024, from https://moodyap.pbworks.com/f/frost.EducationByPoetry.pdf.

———. (1939). The figure a poem makes. In Robert Frost, *Collected poems of Robert Frost*. Holt, Rinehart, and Winston.

Furnham, A., Hughes, D. J., & Marshall, E. (2013). Creativity, OCD, narcissism and the big five. *Thinking Skills and Creativity, 10*, 91–98.

Gil, N. (2019, March 15). Greta Thunberg: The sixteen-year-old climate activist who's become a global celebrity. *Refinery29*. https://www .refinery29.com/en-gb/2019/03/227091/greta-thunberg-climate-strike -nobel-peace-prize.

Gilbert, E. (2016). *Big magic*. Bloomsbury Publishing.

Granneman, J. & Sólo, A. (2023). *Sensitive: The hidden power of the highly sensitive person in a loud, fast, too-much world*. Harmony.

———. (2020, November 30). Biology of OCD [Video]. International OCD Foundation. YouTube. https://www.youtube.com/watch?v=b-2fi UXbq_8.

Green, J. (2014). *The fault in our stars*. Penguin Random House Australia.

———. (2017). *Turtles all the way down*. Penguin USA.

———. (2018, October 4). John Green on how he deals with obsessive-compulsive disorder and "thought spirals." *60 Minutes*. YouTube. https://www.youtube.com/watch?v=r5mdkKYa-fA.

Hamburg, J. (Director). (2009). *I love you, man* [Film]. Paramount Pictures.

Hershfield, J., & Corboy, T. (2013). *The mindfulness workbook for OCD: A guide to overcoming obsessions and compulsions using mindfulness and cognitive behavioral therapy.* New Harbinger.

Hess, A. (2021, May 18). Sinead O'Connor remembers things differently. *New York Times.* https://www.nytimes.com/2021/05/18/arts/music/sinead-oconnor-rememberings.html.

Howard, R. (Director). (2001). *A beautiful mind* [Film]. Universal Pictures.

Jackson, M. (2023). *Uncertain: The wisdom and wonder of being unsure.* Prometheus Books.

Jamison, K. R. (2006). *An unquiet mind.* Alfred A. Knopf.

Jansen, M., Overgaauw, S., & de Bruijn, E. R. (2020). Social cognition and obsessive-compulsive disorder: A review of subdomains of social functioning. *Frontiers in Psychiatry, 11.* https://doi.org/10.3389/fpsyt.2020.00118.

Jonze, S. (Director). (2009). *Where the wild things are* [Film]. Warner Brothers.

Jung, C. G. (1953). *The collected works of Carl Jung.* Pantheon.

Kafka, F. (2014). *The metamorphosis* (S. Bernofsky, Trans.). Norton.

Kalsched, D. (1996). *The inner world of trauma: Archetypal defense of the personal spirit.* Routledge.

———. (2013). *Trauma and the soul: A psycho-spiritual approach to human development.* Routledge.

Keltner, D. (2009, February 12). Darwin's Touch: Survival of the Kindest. *Greater Good Magazine.* https://greatergood.berkeley.edu/article/time/darwins_touch_survival_of_the_kindest.

Keltner, D. (2024). *Awe: The new science of everyday wonder and how it can transform your life.* Penguin Books.

Kerouac, J. (2018). *On the road.* Penguin.

Kochar, N., Ip, S., Vardanega, V., Sireau, N. T., & Fineberg, N. A. (2023). A cost-of-illness analysis of the economic burden of obsessive-compulsive disorder in the United Kingdom. *Comprehensive Psychiatry.* DOI: 10.1016/j.comppsych.2023.152422.

Kross, E. (2021). *Chatter.* Random House United Kingdom.

Langer, E. J. (1997). *The power of mindful learning.* Perseus.

Lansky, S. (2017, June 7). Some people make songs. Jack Antonoff prays for them. *Time.* https://time.com/4806737/jack-antonoff-bleachers-interview/.

Lawrence, D. (1913). Piano. Poetry Foundation. https://www.poetryfoundation.org/poems/44580/piano.

Lewin, R. (1997). *Creative collaboration in psychotherapy: Making room for life.* Jason Aronson.

Lock, S. (2022, October 11). "It felt like a funeral": William Shatner reflects on voyage to space. *The Guardian.* https://www.theguardian.com /culture/2022/oct/11/it-felt-like-a-funeral-william-shatner-reflects -on-voyage-to-space.

MacGuill, D. (2021, March 9). Did Franz Kafka invent letters from a missing doll to comfort a little girl? *Snopes.* Retrieved February 28, 2024, from https://www.snopes.com/fact-check/franz-kafka-doll-girl-story/.

Mills, K., McKay, D., & Chatterjee, U. (2023, October). OCD myths and realities, with Dean McKay, PhD, and Uma Chatterjee [Audio podcast episode no. 260]. *Speaking of Psychology* [Podcast]. American Psychological Association. https://www.apa.org/news/podcasts/speak ing-of-psychology/obsessive-compulsive-disorder.

Mitchell, S. (1988). *Relational concepts in psychoanalysis: An integration.* Harvard University Press.

Moodie, P. (2023). *The joy thief: How OCD steals your happiness—and how to get it back.* Allen & Unwin.

Nicely, S. (2018). *Is Fred in the refrigerator?: Taming OCD and reclaiming my life.* Nicely Done, LLC.

Nyhus, R., & Brumwell, S. C. (2022). *Waving* [Film]. Tanktop films.

OCD Action. (Host). (2022, April 8). *The OCD Stories* podcast with Catherine Benfield, joint virtual conference 2021 [Video podcast episode]. *The OCD Stories* [Podcast]. YouTube. https://www.youtube .com/watch?v=qy13GSMxPT4.

———. (Host). (2023, October 8). Melissa Mose: Internal family systems therapy and ERP [Video podcast episode]. *The OCD Stories* [Podcast]. YouTube. https://theocdstories.com/episode/melissa-402/.

OCD-UK. (2022a). Charles Darwin. OCD UK. https://www.ocduk.org /ocd/history-of-ocd/charles-darwin/#:~:text=Darwin%20also%20 craved%20reassurance%20from,part%20of%20an%20OCD%20 compulsion.

———. (2022b). Nikola Tesla. https://www.ocduk.org/ocd/history-of-ocd /nikola-tesla/#:~:text=It's%20reported%20that%20Tesla%20started, to%20start%20over%20from%20zero.

O'Dunne, Katie [@revkrunsbeyondocd] (2023a, September 2). Does it ever feel like OCD says that you're guilty until proven innocent?! It does for me! [Tweet]. Twitter.

————. [@revkrunsbeyondocd] (2023b, September 9). Intrusive thoughts are just like junk mail. [Tweet]. Twitter.

Ong, C. W., Clyde, J. W., Bluett, E. J., Levin, M. E., & Twohig, M. P. (2016). Dropout rates in exposure with response prevention for obsessive-compulsive disorder: What do the data really say? *Journal of Anxiety Disorders, 40*, 8–17. https://doi.org/10.1016/j.janxdis.2016.03.006.

Overbaugh, J. [@jenna.overbaught] (2023, September 10). Nothing in your content needs to be paid attention to. Nada zilch. [Tweet]. Twitter.

Pastan, L. (1998). *Carnival evening: New and selected poems 1968–1998*. Norton.

Paulson, M. (2020, July 6). Nick Cordero, nominated for tony as tap-dancing tough guy, dies at 41. *New York Times*. https://www.nytimes.com/2020/07/05/obituaries/nick-cordero-dead-coronavirus.html.

Porter, D. (Director). (2020). *John Lewis: Good trouble* [Film]. Magnolia Pictures.

Powers, R. (2021). *Bewilderment*. Norton.

Raimi, S. (Director). (2002). *Spider-Man* [Film]. Sony Pictures.

Raskin, A. (2022). *Overthinking about you: Navigating romantic relationships when you have anxiety, OCD, and/or depression*. Workman.

————. (2023a, October 10). Who would I be without OCD? *Emotional Support Lady*. https://emotionalsupportlady.substack.com/p/who-would-i-be-without-ocd.

————. (2023b, May 30). Why am I like this? A (forced) exploration of my psyche. *Emotional Support Lady*. https://emotionalsupportlady.substack.com/p/why-am-i-like-this.

Real, T. [@realterryreal] (2023, August 12). We human beings cannot be surgical with our feelings. If you open up to one feeling, they all come. [Tweet]. Twitter.

Reiner, R. (Director). (1984). *This is spinal tap* [Film]. Embassy Pictures.

Rockwell-Evans, K. (2023). *Breaking the rules of OCD: Find lasting freedom from the unwanted thoughts, rituals, and compulsions that rule your life*. New Harbinger Publications.

Roddenberry, G. (Creator). (1966–1969). *Star Trek* [Television series]. Paramount Global.

Sacks, O. (1990). *The man who mistook his wife for a hat and other clinical tales*. Harper Perennial.

Salazar Kämpf, M., Kanske, P., Kleiman, A., Haberkamp, A., Glombiewski, J., & Exner, C. (2021). Empathy, compassion, and theory of mind in obsessive-compulsive disorder. *Psychology and Psychotherapy: Theory, Research and Practice, 95*(1), 1–17. https://doi.org/10.1111/papt.12358.

Sendak, M. (1984). *Where the wild things are.* Harper & Row.

Schwartz, M. (2017). *The possibility principle: How quantum physics can improve the way you think, live, and love.* Sounds True.

Schwartz, R. C., & Sweezy, M. (2019). *Internal family systems therapy* (2nd ed.). Guilford Publications.

Shakespeare, W. (2015). *The collected works of William Shakespeare.* Pergamonmedia.

Siegel, Daniel J. (2010). *Mindsight: The new science of personal transformation.* Bantam.

Smith, E. E. (2021, June 24). We want to travel and party. Hold that thought. *New York Times.* https://www.nytimes.com/2021/06/24/opinion/covid-pandemic-grief.html.

Smith, E. (2023, December 5). Personal communication with the author.

Smith, W. K., & Lewis, M. W. (2022). *Both/and thinking: Embracing creative tensions to solve your toughest problems.* Harvard Business Review Press.

Spielberg, S. (Director). (2022). *The fabelmans* [Film]. Universal.

Stern, D. B. (2009). *Partners in thought: Working with unformulated experience, dissociation, and enactment.* Routledge.

Stulberg, B. (2023). *Master of change: How to excel when everything is changing—including you.* HarperOne.

Styron, W. (1992). *Sophie's choice.* Vintage.

Szymborska, W., Barańczak, S., & Cavanagh, C. (2000). *Poems, new and collected*, 1957–1997. San Diego: Harcourt Brace.

Tapper, J. (2020, February 22). Greta Thunberg's mother reveals teenager's troubled childhood. *The Guardian.* https://www.theguardian.com/environment/2020/feb/22/greta-thunberg-mother-she-stopped-talking-and-eating.

Tawwab, N. G. (2021). *Set boundaries, find peace: A guide to reclaiming yourself.* TarcherPerigee, an imprint of Penguin Random House LLC.

Valiunas, A. (Fall 2009–Winter 2010). Darwin's world of pain and wonder. *New Atlantis* (Fall 2009-Winter 2010), n.p. https://www.thenewatlantis.com/publications/darwins-world-of-pain-and-wonder.

Wachtel, P. (1993). *Therapeutic communication: Knowing what to say when.* Guilford.

Washington, P. (Ed.). (2006). *Rumi poems* (Everyman's Library Pocket Book ed.). Alfred A. Knopf.

Weinberger, J. (2023, May 23). The unconscious is not what you think it is: TEDxIrvington. TEDxTalks. YouTube. https://www.youtube.com/watch?v=W4C8wfShGTg.

Weinberger, J., & Stoycheva, V. (2021). *Unconscious: Theory, research, and clinical implications*. Guilford.

Weiss, D. (2015, June 24). How bleachers' Jack Antonoff survives summer festivals with OCD. *Spin*. https://www.spin.com/2015/06/jack-antonoff-bleachers-summer-festival-ocd-shadow-of-the-city/.

Whitman, W. (2002). *Leaves of grass and other writings* (M. Moon, Ed.). Norton.

Wilson, M. (2016). *Where am I now?: True stories of girlhood and accidental fame*. Penguin Books.

Wilson, S. (2019). *First, we make the beast beautiful*. Random House United Kingdom.

Wilson, T. [@tortillawilson] (2023, October 14). We are so good at "solving away" our emotion. That's what my OCD journey has been all about. [Tweet]. Twitter.

Wolf, D. (Executive Producer). (1990–). *Law & order* [TV series].

Women's Agenda. (2023, September 19). Penny Moodie unpacks OCD in new book, *The Joy Thief*. Books, *Women's Agenda*. https://womensagenda.com.au/life/books/penny-moodie-unpacks-ocd-in-new-book-the-joy-thief/.

Ziegler, S., Bednasch, K., Baldofski, S., & Rummel-Kluge, C. (2021). Long durations from symptom onset to diagnosis and from diagnosis to treatment in obsessive-compulsive disorder: A retrospective self-report study. *PLOS One*, *16*(12). https://doi.org/10.1371/journal.pone.0261169.

Zlotowitz, M., & Scherman, N. (Eds.). (1999). *Pirkei avos: ethics of the fathers (Artscroll Mesorah Series)*. Mesorah Publications.

INDEX

ABOUT THE AUTHOR

Michael Alcée, PhD, is a clinical psychologist in private practice in Tarrytown, NY, and is a Mental Health Educator at the Manhattan School of Music. He is the author of *Therapeutic Improvisation: How to Stop Winging It and Own It as a Therapist*. Michael was the winner of the American Psychological Association's Division 39 Schillinger Memorial Award in 2019 for the best essay on the link between psychoanalysis and jazz. He is a regular contributor at *Psychology Today* where he writes about the intersection between creativity, psychotherapy, parenting, improv, pop culture, and much more. Michael has contributed to *NPR*, *The Chicago Tribune*, and *The New York Times*, among others. He has been a TEDx speaker and organizer and has appeared on a variety of podcasts.